THE CAPTAIN'S

Mary

THE ROAD TO FENHAM FARM

MARY BYERS MCNABB

Copyright © 2016

Mary Byers McNabb
The Captain's Mary
The Road to Fenham Farm

PB: ISBN 978-0-9952895-0-5

Cover Art: Original oil painting by Mary Byers McNabb

Published and Printed in Canada

*Dedicated to
the five generations
of our family
whose vision
and hard work
have made the dream
of Fenham
a reality*

Byers Family Crest

Foreword

My sister and I grew up in a large, sprawling house filled with the relics of our family's story. Fenham was home to a very large family, many of whom lived far away and yet they made their pilgrimages home. Stories were told, memories were shared and familial bonds were strengthened.

Sometimes the family gatherings were joyous times of celebration but too often it seemed they were times of mourning. It seemed to us that every member of our family who died was brought back to Fenham. Time and again, the deceased loved one was laid out in the front parlour and relatives and friends flocked to our home to pay their respects.

What was it about our home that everyone had to come to in life and in death? There was something mysterious, intangible and magnetic about our home. People we barely knew were drawn to it. What was common to all of them, and to us, was that we were the descendants of Captain William Byers and his wife Mary Dudderidge.

Time and time again we heard the stories of the Captain's dream to build Fenham in the Canadian wilderness. We were regaled with the tragic tale of his untimely death and the subsequent hardships the family endured until finally, with much hard work, Mary and her family carved out our farm, our home, making Captain William's dream come true for all of us.

And so it was that Fenham was a shrine to our family's heritage. Over the years fewer and fewer people knew the stories. Would the story be lost, especially when the family left Fenham and relatives stopped coming home? We wondered.

Just as we were leaving Fenham we discovered the extensive collection of letters that Mary Dudderidge Byers, and others, had carefully preserved. When finally we found the time and the energy to delve into the letters, we began to know our ancestors in new and exciting ways.

My sister Mary, who has always been my dear, dear friend, has done an excellent job of bringing Mary and William's story to life. *The Captain's Mary* is a great read. William and Mary tell their own stories. We feel their emotions, we sense their trials and we revel in their triumphs. It is a tale of struggle and determination and it is a story we cherish and proudly share.

Willian R. Byers

August, 2016

Mary Dudderidge Byers
(Photo by Notman & Son, Montreal)

Mary Dudderidge Byers
Fenham Farm, West Hawkesbury, Ontario 1873

The breeze is light. The ripened wheat in the front field waves its golden hues, a sea of motion in the late afternoon sun. Soothed by the rhythm of the golden sea, Mary, now in her eighties, sits to rest and enjoy the splendour, the brilliance of the late September colour. From her rocking chair on the front veranda, the rolling Laurentian Hills, the mountains that have caused so many tears, now resplendent in all their glory, say "peace."

She is peaceful. Life has been a journey of happiness and sorrow, with hardships beyond belief, but one that has brought her to this beautiful home, the culmination of her dreams. She knows that William must be very proud of what she and her children have accomplished.

In her hand she opens a small, red leather case. The oval glass protects a small miniature of her beloved William. He was so young and handsome in his dark mariner's uniform. She remembers how worried she had been when news from a terrible storm told her of the loss of his right eye. Gazing at his face she sees no imperfection. Only courage and love speak to her. She turns it over to admire again the tiny pearls that surround the lock of his dark hair, a curl that reminds her of the soft caring man who left her so long ago.

She has had a busy day. There was a time when it would have been difficult to imagine that someday she would do only what she wanted to do but now she was doing just that. Her head starts to nod, her eyes are very heavy, her faithful blue jay calls and she sleeps.

(Byers Family Collection)

1

Prologue

When you are young thoughts of long ago seldom enter your mind. Age helps you to appreciate who you are and where you have come from. I grew up at Fenham Farm, a beautiful home with a fantastic history. The stately house on the hill overlooked a busy barnyard dominated by a gigantic cattle barn replete with a fish weathervane on the peak of its clerestory roof. Golden Guernsey cows dotted the field behind the barn. Crystal clear spring water supplied the barns and flowed through the water trough ensuring that no animal ever had to go thirsty. The same, cold, sparkling water supplied the house as well as the water fountain, the focal point of the manicured front lawn.

The Dooryard at Fenham Farm overlooking the farmstead – 1940's
(Byers family collection)

The Fountain at Fenham
(Byers family collection)

Fenham Farm was a beautiful world for my older sister, Ruth and me. Outside, at play, we always felt safe. We had our white haired Grandpa and a big, golden collie dog named Sailor to care for us. We were our Grandpa's two little shadows as he puttered about building interesting structures with his carefully collected stones. With an eye out for us he tended his rock gardens and mowed the lawns. The hill to the barnyard was a challenge. It was not unusual to see Billy the pony hitched to the lawn mower with Grandpa on the reins.

Grandpa always seemed to be carting something around in his wheelbarrow. Often it was us. We were very lucky little girls. He passed away on January 1, 1944, but he's still an angel on my shoulder when I sit and write at his old desk. Sadly, my brother Bill and my little sister Anne never knew this kind, loving old gentleman.

At an early age we knew that, long ago, our ancestors had crossed the Atlantic Ocean on a sailing ship called the Success and that, somehow, these people had carved "our Fenham Farm" out of the Canadian wilderness. As a reminder of our heritage the big bell saved from the ship Success hung in the belfry on top of the carriage house. At meal times the bell was rung to call Dad and the hired men in from the fields. If an emergency required Dad's attention the bell was tolled - a signal to come at once.

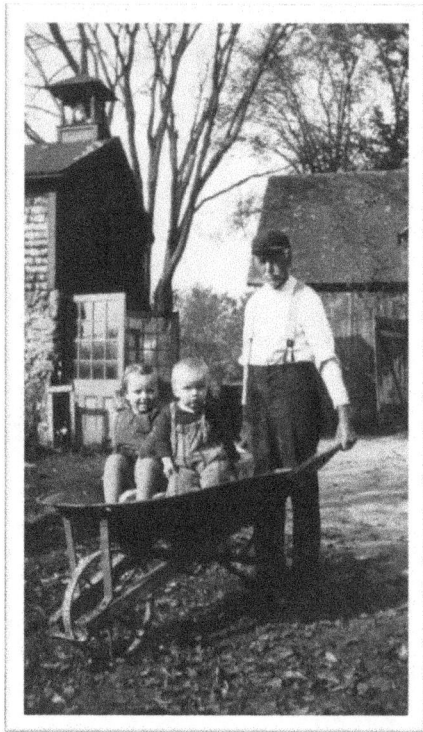

Ruth & Mary in Grandpa's wheelbarrow (Byers Family Collection)

Ship's Bell - The Success 1803 (Photo by John Byers)

We knew that the little, framed, black and white silhouettes that hung in a cluster on the dining room wall were pictures of people who had sailed on that ship, but we never knew their names. A strange little table sat nestled against the ancient grandfather clock. If you lifted the top it was easily transformed into a washstand. This was no ordinary washstand. It was a piece of ship's furniture that had accompanied our great-great-grandfather, Captain William Byers, on his many sea voyages. Its small drawer held tiny skeletons of birds, rocks, bones and shells that we knew we must not touch. They were history and must be cared for.

4

We all grew up, times changed, the bottom fell out of the cheddar cheese market and the farm was sold. Memories of five generations of the Byers family had to be sorted, kept, claimed, given away or sold. My brother, Bill, and I were given the daunting task of cleaning out the upper floor of the old workshop. We carted down weaving frames, spinning wheels, old chairs, stools, picture frames, churns, an old wicker baby carriage and much, much more, all adorned with a generous layer of dust

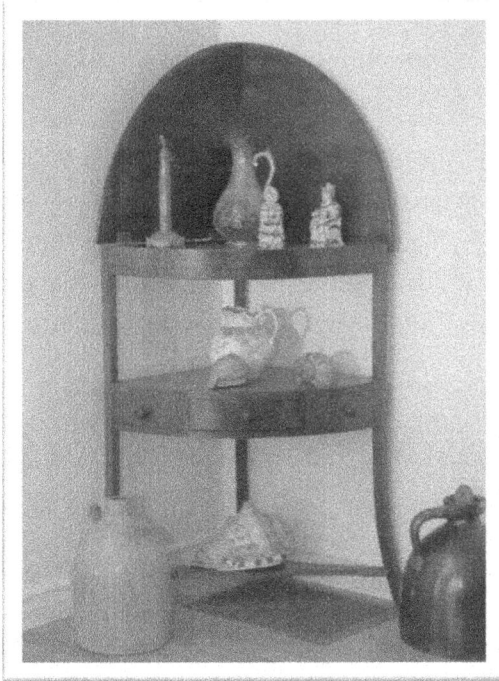

The ship's washstand
(Photo by John Byers)

We came upon an interesting, old box. It was heavy but made no sound when we shook it. We opened it carefully to discover that it was crammed with old family letters and documents that someone had cherished, saved and brought from England. It turned out to be a gold mine of family history - a treasure that most people could only dream of having. For my brother, who already knew much of the story and had some old letters, it was a windfall.

The Letters

From that time on the letters, along with others acquired from a cousin, were lovingly cared for, catalogued and finally transcribed by my brother. There were so many of them that it took hours and hours of concentrated work to decipher the secrets enclosed in the fragile pages, often hidden within the idiosyncrasies of questionable handwriting. The Byers family owes him a sincere thank you for his efforts. When he gave me the copy of his work I can truthfully say, that as a present, it could only be surpassed by the gift of my daughters and five grandchildren.

The first letter of the collection is dated Sept. 27, 1794. It is the only surviving letter written by our great-great-great-great-grandmother, Margaret Dudderidge, who lived in the Dudderidge home in Bridgwater, Somerset, England. Others dating from 1805 to 1833, relate the way of life and the personalities of the characters that make up the first part of the family story.

Mary Dudderridge, our great-great-grandmother, is the central character in this story. Many letters reveal the loving relationship she shared with her mother, Elizabeth Clarkson Dudderidge Huxtable. Their closely-knit bond reveals a relationship built upon mutual love and respect.

More insight is gained from the letters written by James (Jem) and Edward (Ned) Dudderidge, Mary's brothers, two slightly spoiled younger siblings, whose prime reason for writing is to get their mother and sister to give them something they want. We watch them grow up, marry and struggle to find their places in the world.

The letters also reveal another interesting family member, the Reverend William Clarkson, a Roman Catholic priest and Carmelite monk. He is Elizabeth Clarkson Dudderidge Huxtable's brother. It was challenging for Roman Catholics to openly practice their faith in England at the time. After several years in Liege Belgium where he had a parish church, he returned to England to escape the onslaught of Napoleon's army. In England he served as chaplain and enjoyed the generosity of wealthy Roman Catholic families.

Mary's story takes a dramatic turn in 1815 when she meets a dashing young Sea Captain, William Byers. They fall in love, soon marry and form a partnership that provides a firm foundation and lasting legacy for generations yet to come. Their correspondence is rich and revealing, filled with romance, disappointment, and the ebb and flow of daily life.

Through the Captain we meet his mother, Ann Nicholson Byers, and his sister, Dorothy Byers Thompson, and members of her family. Other writers, business colleagues, salty seamen, and friends help to give us glimpses into the lives of the main characters and into life in the 1800's. The letters written by Mary Dudderidge Byers and William Byers to each other are the backbone of this true historical composition.

Life and Times

Britain has always been a very proud nation but never more so than when Lord Nelson, at the Battle of Trafalgar in 1805, put an end to the Napoleonic Wars at sea. Britain was now "Mistress of the Seas" again.

Due to improved hygiene in the late 1700's and early 1800's, London, by 1815, had become the island's largest city with a population of one and a quarter million. This era was intellectually labelled the Age of Enlightenment. The idea of the value of the common person and the power of human reasoning to overcome the problems of the world led to conflict between the young and the old. Education for girls was now a normal happening. Working and peasant girls went to Primary School to learn the basic 3R's while the middle class and aristocrats attended private secondary schools gaining a much wider education. Social skills and needlework were very important for these young ladies.

Music was now to be written for the enjoyment of the common folk not for just the church and court. Public concerts became an important part of the musical scene. Cricket was the game in fashion for many. It was, indeed, a classical era with the rise of the middle class and capitalism.

Away from London the geography of an area was the main factor in determining the people's way of life. County Kent with its harbours had been the front line of many conflicts. England had relied on the country's many northern and southern ports to provide shipbuilding and dockage for war ships for more than eight hundred years. In the 19th century the smuggling of spirits, tobacco and salt from France and the same for wool back to France was very much a problem for those who called the coast their home.

Away from the docks rich fields of orchards and hops surrounded an active commercial community. Ships from the West Indies brought much needed sugar, molasses and rum to be either taken by ship to London and the interior or to the north, to Newcastle and the South Shields area. Manufactured goods from the north left the southern ports bound for the Indies or the continent. It was a very busy part of southern England.

With all this activity there were always people coming or going. Many needed a place to stay for a night or two. The Fountain Inn, a landmark along the Thames was a coach house owned and operated by the Clarkson family of Sheerness, on the Isle of Sheppey. It is, in fact, where our story begins.

Sheerness, Kent, England, 1814

The breeze is light. The waves, sparkling in the morning sun, lap at the Sheerness sea wall. A young woman sits and dreams. Mary, at twenty three, is restless. But why? There is music all around her, the music of her life. Sea birds call, swoop and strut in search of breakfast. The riggings of the ships' masts strain and bow to the impatient winds. Waiting, yet again to sail away, they tell tales of stormy seas past and dream of adventures yet to come.

In the picture on the following page, the Fountain Inn is in the center of the picture, the tall building, behind the flag pole

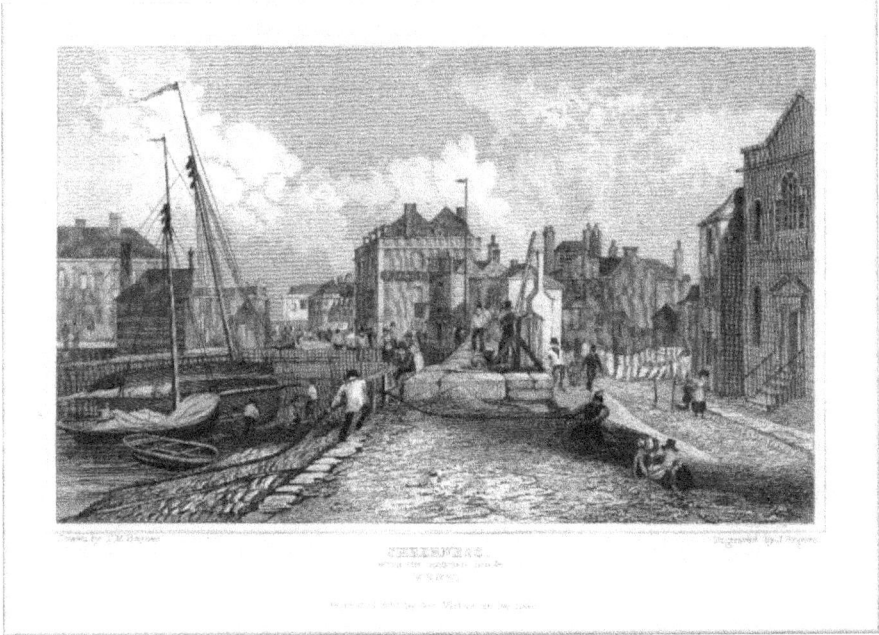

The Fountain Inn, Sheerness, Kent, England

(London: George Virtue, 1830. Antique print, engraved by John Rogers (1800?-1882) from an original study by the landscape printer Thomas Mann Baynes. Originally produced for the "England's Topograher" series of kent Views (London : 1828-1831, copyright expired, print used with permission of owner, John Byers)

On the opposite dock a crew is preparing to set sail. The commanding voice of the captain catches her attention. He is young and handsome, not grey haired and whiskered as she had imagined. She watches as he meticulously and effortlessly finishes the preparations. The ropes are cast off and smoothly his brig heads out to sea. She likes its name, the Langley, and she finds herself wondering about the Captain.

She has seen this young captain before. Most captains are older, weather beaten and grey, not youthful and in command at such an early age. She remembers that her mother buys sugar, molasses and rum when this ship returns from Antigua. He is interesting, very interesting. Quietly she watches and listens. As the scene unfolds she does not notice that the young captain is also watching her. He wonders where her dreams are taking her, why she is alone at this time of day and who she is. The brig glides by, the captain smiles, touches his hat and vows that when he returns he will get to know the pretty, young lass who sits and watches and dreams.

She is restless and wonders why. Her life flashes before her. She has a good life, a loving family and many friends. A big part of her life has been devoted to helping her mother, Elizabeth, in the daily commercial life of the Fountain Inn. From its prominent location on the High Street of Sheerness, the old, weatherworn inn has, for over a century, faithfully served as a hostel and carriage house.

Built in 1700 and owned by her mother's brother, George Clarkson, it is ideally located with an easy view of the docks and serves as a home base for the people of the sea and those who call Sheerness and the Isle of Sheppey their home. It is a comfortable, three storey, red brick building that houses family and travellers from land or sea.

Elizabeth Clarkson Dudderidge Huxtable is the Inn's hostess. At Saint Leonard's, Shoreditch, London, November 20th, 1788 she had married a Somerset man named Richard Dudderidge. Sadly he died when her three children were young. She married again. With Anthony Huxtable, a Minster man, she had a daughter, Elizabeth, who, not being strong, had passed away at an early age in 1807. The child was followed by her father in 1808.

Mary is proud of her strong, compassionate mother. The dark carved woodwork of the Fountain Inn, softened by the warmth of candlelight, creates an ambience that with the warmth of Elizabeth, more than anything else, encourages the visitor to sit and enjoy the fellowship and conversation of the hour.

Like the Inn, Elizabeth has been around a long time. She is greatly loved by the people. In many ways she is the Fountain Inn. Elizabeth is also wise. She has made sure that, if need be, Mary is capable of filling her shoes.

Mary's eyes fill with tears as she remembers losing her little step-sister, Elizabeth. Not being home to support her mother at the burial on November 10, 1807, had been a day like no other. She had been at Tusmore and her brothers were away at school, at Sedgley Park, when her mother's letter arrived with the dreaded news and money to buy mourning clothes. She still wondered why her step-father had gone to Tusmore to be with her Uncle William, leaving his wife to grieve alone. He had been a hard man, not easy to understand.

Watching the waves she remembers how brother James, in July 1809, narrowly escaped death when he and two pals engaged a sailboat, got caught in a squall and overturned, leaving only two of the three to reach shore safely. It seemed to make him grow up and, much to his mother's relief, two years later he found work in the linen and clothing business.

Her thoughts then turn to Edward. Ned, the baby of the Dudderidge family, has not easily found his calling. As a school boy he soon learned that Mary was a soft touch. He constantly asks her, not his mother, for money and most often he gets it. Being the youngest of the family seems to have its advantages. Now he has apprenticed to be a surgeon/chemist but is having difficulty getting established and is still a worry to his mother and sister.

Both boys stepped gingerly around their step-father, Anthony Huxtable. Their mother's admonition to refrain from telling him when she is giving them money suggests he has a stern, less compassionate side to his character.

Life with these two boys is never dull. She loves them dearly but hopes that they will soon be totally independent with productive lives of their own.

Her memories flash back to visits with her grandmother, Mary Nivum Clarkson, where on Well Street, Well-Close Square she had played with friends and Clarkson cousins in the streets of London. Her grandmother had taught her to make french knots, delicate stitches that she now uses in so much of her needlework. At eleven years of age she had proudly played secretary while writing letters for her grandmother to her Uncle William.

Visits with her other grandmother, Margaret Dudderidge, who ran a boarding house in Bridgwater in Somerset were just as memorable. So many wonderful stories; one, a tale of how the citizenry of Bridgwater had armed the town with a volunteer force to repel the French if they should happen to invade, was of particular interest. She was lucky to have known two loving grandmothers. All such good memories!

Suddenly, she realizes that she has been dreaming too long. She has needlework to finish for Mr. King for his shop on Grosvenor Square. Ten years of being her Uncle William's housekeeper at Tusmore have given her many good friends that she must not neglect. She must answer their letters. Reluctantly she gets to her feet.

The music is still around her. A gust of wind cries through ropes as they strain against their relentless ties to the wall. A loose sail flaps, a flag cries for freedom, a stray barrel rolls without restraint, a sailor's song and the chime of a bell complete the scale. She really has nothing to complain about. She cannot sail away, she must get back to work.

Meanwhile, going out to sea, young Captain Byers is thinking about the pretty young lady sitting in the morning sun. He has been alone too long. He had loved Ann, his wife of so short a time. In 1809 she had given him a daughter, Elizabeth, or Eliza as she was fondly known. Sadly their second child had not lived and Ann had sunk into a deep depression. Too soon he had convinced her to accompany him on his next voyage to Antigua. It had not been a wise decision on both their parts. Far from their northern coastal home of South Shields, off the coast of Spain, she became ill and tragically she died. He did what he had to do and buried her, alone, in Cadiz, Spain. He had to go on. He had no choice.

He yearns for a new, loving companion. Little Elizabeth needs a caring mother. How he longs for another love to fill the void. On his return he resolves to find the beauty by the pier, the little lass who was stealing his heart as he sailed away. He prays for fair winds and following seas and a very, very short voyage to Antigua and back.

Mary's Uncle William

In England, during the reigns of King George III and King George IV it is still difficult to be a Roman Catholic. The Clarksons are devout followers of the Roman faith. Elizabeth's brother, William Clarkson, is a Carmelite priest, a monk, a member of a monastic community in Liege, Belgium.

The Rev. William Clarkson
(Byers family collection)

The destruction of the French Revolution and the Napoleonic Wars has left Europe in a state of uncertainty. Many religious communities, for safety sake, have disbanded with the scattered members forced to settle in smaller, safer communities. William Clarkson has returned to England to the company and safety of his family and friends. Here he finds a new ministry and a new flock to pastor at Tusmore, Northamptonshire, serving as chaplain on the estate of the Fermore family, a wealthy Roman Catholic family, who have been able to practice their religion in relative peace. Security is ensured by a *"priestly hiding hole"* where the resident cleric can hide if the authorities come seeking out religious indiscretions. A connecting tunnel guarantees a speedy escape.

At Tusmore, Mary spends a great deal of time as companion and housekeeper to her Uncle William. Here she lives a somewhat privileged life though never really able to break the servant/master barrier. In this *"upstairs downstairs"* atmosphere she is befriended by Catherine Fermore, the daughter of the house. Together they spend relaxed times, doing needlework, playing cards and visiting together and through the community.

Frequently Catherine remembers who she is and in a flash Mary is expected to do some service for her friend. With good humour she serves and enjoys her companion. The glass ceiling is difficult to break but life is fun while it lasts and the life style is fascinating.

13

From 1066 to 1828 several generations of Fermores have lived, as Lords of the Manor, on the 735 acre estate. Today only the dovecote, a house for doves, elevated on ancient staddle stones remains. Staddle stones support bases for granaries and hayricks allowing the structure and its contents to be elevated above the ground to prevent damage from rodents, damp and mould. In 1770 William Fermore demolished most of the ancient house and replaced it with an unpretentious russet and grey stone Italianate villa. The old chapel was retained by building it into the new parlour. Beautiful grounds, including a lake, a red brick walled garden, with surrounding hedges accent this impressive mansion. Two tenant farms, Chaise Bain and Pimlico, assure the viability of Tusmore Park.

The Rev. William Clarkson's duty at Tusmore is to attend to the spiritual needs of the Fermore family and to the families working and living on the estate. They too cannot openly practice their faith. For this service and when he accompanies them on vacation to Margate by the Sea, "*to take the waters*" their faithful priest celebrates the Mass and tends to their spiritual needs. He serves them well and in return he and his niece, Mary, live a very comfortable life. He is often an honoured guest with those who come for tea, musical entertainment and dinner. In fact, it is a sign of status to have a resident priest and chaplain.

Mary, on the other hand, takes her meals *"downstairs."* Here with the house keeper and friendly servants Mary finds her real, true friends. Mrs. Collingridge from the nearby village of Hardwick, presides over the domestic life of Tusmore and for many years keeps Mary up to date with long newsy letters.

Mary has only one wish. She wants a family of her own. She's dreaming again! Oh for a holiday!

One Wish Comes True

Napoleon's pugilistic folly has come to an end. William Clarkson is worried about his brother priests in war torn Liege. How have they and the few remaining sisters survived the cruelty of the Prussian soldiers? To ease his mind he must go to the continent. His health is not the best and he is hesitant to travel alone. He so enjoys the company of his niece and the security she affords him. He is certain her mother will not refuse his appeal to have Mary accompany him, so he begins to make plans.

Promising young ladies of Mary's age often go to the continent in search of interesting suitors, so not surprisingly, Mary is thrilled to go *"en tour."* A whole new world is about to open up. She can hardly wait. She feels that she is well prepared to handle any milieu in which she finds herself.

We know very little of Mary's formal education but from her writings we meet a cultured, young woman whose smooth style and beautiful descriptive phrasing enable us to see what she sees, enjoy what she enjoys and reveals her to be a fashionable, witty, knowledgeable young lady of her time.

A Vast New World

Although she is well chaperoned, life with Uncle William is never dull. With her mother Elizabeth tagging along they set out *"with great expectations"* for the Dover coast. It is a great place to begin. They will *"take the waters"* at Margate and enjoy the clean fresh air while they live in style. The four-storied, terraced beach hotels with dining rooms, assembly rooms and libraries make everyone most welcome.

Elizabeth sees to it that Mary is well dressed for her holiday but Mary still marvels at the fashions all around her. To be sure that she will remember the most popular trends she makes notes. Promenade and evening dresses are long, slim and silky, just sitting on the toe of the shoe. Compulsory accessories are one of either cape, shawl or stole, along with small cloche hat and reticule. Walking dresses are slim, showing the shoe, topped off with a knee length overcoat and completed with a hat and umbrella. Sports dresses are slim and short sleeved for comfort in the sun. Beach wear is very modest, short sleeved, mid-calf, bathing cap and water shoes.

Mary, like all young ladies, can never know too much about the latest fashion trends.

After a few days of fun by the sea they are anxious to be on their way. To relax and rest Elizabeth is to stay on with her friends. Promising to faithfully write her mother, on July 16th, 1814, *"about nine in the evening with a fair wind,"* uncle and niece set out by the Ostend Packet to cross the English Channel to the allure of the continent.

Having never before crossed the Channel the experience of sailing in a boat with side sleeping bunks and centre tables and benches fascinates her. People are resting, visiting and some are even playing cards.

> *"Some of the ladies were ill, but I remained in bed, neither ate nor drank anything and thus escaped the worst of the travelling troubles. It was a very pleasant journey."*

They safely reach the shores of Belgium about 8 o'clock the next morning only to find their first stop to be disappointing.

> *"It is a very poor place, but remarkably, provisions very plentiful and cheap, the finest fowls one shilling apiece and everything else in proportion. I like the manner of cooking very much, tho' not their wines. Suppose I have had a bad taste, but they appear to me sour."*

They remain in Ostend only long enough to dine and then proceed by canal barge to Bruges.

> *"You need not laugh at this, for I believe there is not an hotel in London with half the accommodations we have on board, and most delightfully pleasant, the canal being cut through one of the finest countries you can imagine, and our party being the same as that came from Margate, there being a few strangers added to it.*

*I met with the kindest attention from Mrs. Ferguson who was
coming with her husband to join his regiment at Brussels. Capt. F.
is a very pleasant gentleman; Dr. & Mrs. Jones, Colonel Darvil of
the Guards, Admiral Donnelly, all very gentlemanly, etc. etc., but
Mrs. F. is one of the handsomest women I ever met.*

*Well, we arrived at Bruges about eight in the evening and had a
walk round the town. It appeared very sombre, and many of the
streets with half the houses let. In short, quite deserted, grass
growing in many places, but very clean. We left this place, but
must say I have not slept in such a comfortable bed since I left
home as I did here. We left Bruges about nine in the morning
Friday, in another barge. This one was fitted up in grander style
with three rooms below. We dined onboard and had the finest fish
dinner I ever sat down to - turbot, eels, cod, soles, and sturgeon,
etc., with beautiful pastry and fruit all served up in grand style.
There being a first and second table, this appeared to me more like
a pleasure trip than travelling."*

With four horses to pull the barge they travel slowly arriving in Ghent
about five in the evening. They transfer to the *"Hotel of the Low Countries"*
which to Mary was *"almost a castle. Ghent is much more exciting with so
much to see."* A visit to the Cathedral and a ride with Mrs. Jones in a
cabriole allows Mary to mingle with foreigners *"in bonnets, which are,
without joking, full half a yard from their heads and seven or eight full blown
roses on top."* The fashion of the French ladies makes a lasting impression
and will supply fodder for many stories when she returns home.

*"We left Ghent at 11 o'clock Saturday, in the coach, Diligence. The
road from Ghent to Brussels is the most delightful imaginable. You
remember the Grove at Finchley 'tis like that all the way, a
distance of forty miles, and the fields in the finest cultivation."*

The trip is going very well but Mary is a bit disappointed for she has met
with nothing unpleasant yet!

The following Wednesday they leave Brussels by carriage having forsaken
the Diligence *"because Uncle thought that it would be too tiring."* The first

day they travel as far as Louvain only to encounter scenes of despair and carnage. A walk to see a Carmelite church finds only the walls standing; *"those vile Frenchmen having pulled it all down."* The adjoining convent is gone, and in its place is a garden, the remaining building inhabited *"by the lowest order of people."* Two other Carmelite convents, along with many others, have been destroyed. The people of Louvain complain that the town has been ruined by the suppression of the university where formally 3000 students, from different countries, had studied. The Prussian soldiers have done their worst.

Saint Trong is next. There they spend the night and the next day complete their journey to Liege, where Uncle William finds only eight of his friends still living. The wars have left little untouched. *"The Church of St. Lambert, which was one of the finest buildings in the world, and which covered as much ground, I think, as our St. Paul's is quite gone. Nothing but the walls of the Cloisters on one side remain."*

Uncle's church is now a stable, the steps covered with straw, with soldiers lolling at the doors. *"It had been a handsome building. The outside still remains, a melancholy memorial of what it once was. The town is nearly full of Prussian soldiers, who distress the inhabitants very much. They are a swarm of locusts, devouring everything before them."*

It is a most distressing time for the troubled priest. If the soldiers would leave perhaps life could settle down and the people would know to which country they belong. The national boundaries of the post-war period will be re-drawn but as yet no one knows just how. In spite of the turmoil, the town is as bustling as London and provisions are plentiful and cheap. Mary wishes that she could send some of the delicious fruit back to her mother and friends in England.

Mary assures her mother that all is well.

> *"I am very comfortable which I know will give you pleasure to hear. There is a lady here who is particularly kind to me. You would laugh to see us, for she cannot speak a word of English nor I French, and yet we walk out together, but I take good care not to*

lose sight of her as I should be in a pretty situation if I was, do you not think? We are uncommonly good company. I do assure you we are very merry, if not witty.

My dear Uncle is uncommonly good to me. He took me yesterday to see the English College. 'Tis literally falling to pieces, but most beautifully situated on the declivity of a hill. You ascend eighty-five steps to it, and go out of the top of the house to the gardens which are extremely large and beautiful. Oh, such quantities of fruit! The views are beyond description. It is the pleasantest place I saw in my life. The town has a river which, I forget the name of, runs through it and there are a number of bridges built over it. The river forms a canal up which barges come from different places, and even boats without ends or sides on. There is a grand promenade, shaded by bare trees, one in the middle is for carriages and the ones on either side are for pedestrians. On the right is the water and a distant view of the hills. Cottages here and there enliven the scene. To the left is a range of hills covered with vines and a row of houses at the bottom of them. Many of the houses are deserted. They are very noble, indeed all the buildings are superior to those in Brussels."

July 14, 1814, Mary writes again, from Liege, having returned from a trip to Spa and Aix-la-Chapelle where Napoleon had built a fort to ward off an invasion from the British. Mary was prompted to say that Spa is *"too much praised in England, for it is not half so pleasant a place as Liege. There were not more than a dozen English there. We went to the theatre and were much amused. We saw 'Lodvisea Lovers Quarrels.' This is, with the exception of gaming, the only amusement. They adjourn from the theatre to the rooms where they lose their money in style."*

They stayed in Aix-la-Chapelle for ten days. *"It is a gay place, a fashionable watering hole for the nobility and gentry of the country, and the headquarters of the Prussian army. We have had princes, generals, barons and God knows what other titles in our hotel, the first time I have had the honour of dining in such princely company. The ladies dressed very well there, except their bonnets. They never appeared at table twice in the same dress."*

Napoleon is the benefactor of Aix-la-Chapelle. He provides 200,000 francs yearly for the preservation of the baths. His picture and that of the Empress adorn the Town Hall. *"Some of the Royal Family spent part of every summer here. The townspeople tell, with a smile, of the farce Napoleon practised there previous to his Coronation. Before Napoleon's spectacular ceremony, many, including Prince Charlemagne, were crowned in this place. Accordingly, Napoleon and his wife used to command the heads of the Church to frequently meet them at the Church in order to be perfect in the farce which was acted in Paris with all the regalia, etc."*

Mary learns that the Carmelite sisters have fared no better than the brothers. For more than fifteen years they have suffered persecution. Ten nuns and two novices have hidden themselves in various locations. The church is a magazine once used for hops. *"The Carmelite gardens are too beautiful to describe, the Church is a stable, the Convent a magazine."* Mary wonders at their courage and faith. They hope that things will be better when the government of the country is settled. They are so impressive that Mary wishes that she could stay a year with them. They send her away with a gift for her mother.

Thankfully, there is time for fun. She tells her mother about a trip to Chaude Fontaine.

"Tis not more than four leagues from Liege and my Uncle took us, a young lady here who is kind to me, in a chaise. He drove and I was just telling him not to spill us, when lo and behold, a car man, who was coming along without heeding which way his horses turned, let them come suddenly across the road, plump against the wheel of our chaise, with such a jerk as Hercules would have done in the fable, had he complied with his petitioner's request, and tho' I have little gravity in my composition, for the life of me could not keep my seat, so out I popped and as I like good company at all times seized my Uncle's arm and in spite of mademoiselle, who held on to the tail of his coat, I got them both out to great astonishment

of my Uncle, who having the lady on top of him, could only look at me, who was shaking my feathers from the dust very composedly and enquiring if they were hurt, when Mr. C., by a sudden exertion disengaged himself with the loss of one flap of his coat, and lifted us both in again. Off we set to the infinite surprise of the spectators. All this was done in one tenth part of the time I have taken to tell you of it. I could not speak for some time, laughing prevented me. I always am that way inclined when I think how cleverly I handed them both out."

Time is flying by, leaving only a visit to Paris before they must head for home. For Mary the anticipation of a visit to the most famous city in the world blocks out the beauty and calm of the French countryside. Uncle William, looking very tired, is pensive. Hopefully a good night's rest will restore his energy so that he may be able to show her all that he has promised of the much talked about life of Paris.

On arrival it is quite evident that the defeat of Napoleon has not broken the heart of the city. Colourful, fashionable crowds, peppered with the colour of the British military, stroll or ride about with an air of purpose.

For the next few days they play tourist and soak up the ambience of the great city. One great edifice cannot outshine the next. The beauty of the great Cathedral, the mesmerizing treasures of the Louvre, the Palais Royal, the opulence of their accommodations and so much more fills their hours in an exciting new world. Even under the constant eye of Uncle, Mary soon sees that this great city, like all others, has a life of a different colour, a life of gaming, of ladies of the streets and houses of ill repute. She loves it all. Exhausted at the end of the day, she cannot write her daily letters home. How can she put to paper all that she has seen? Her family and friends will just have to wait till can see them in person.

If someone should ask if she has found a husband she will just have to answer that she had had no time to look. Another Packet ride and she is safely home.

Her world had widened considerably by the end of the tour. She had seen natural beauty paralleled by misery, soldiers, chaos, and destruction, all measured against a privileged society of spas, theatre and affluence. How can she ever thank her dear Uncle William for this fantastic holiday and how can she do it justice when she recounts it to her friends?

Captain William Nelson Edward Byers

The autumn of 1814 slips away. Brigs come to port and sail back out to sea. Mary watches and waits, wondering if she will ever see the dashing young captain who tipped his hat and now constantly frequents her dreams.

Meanwhile, in Antigua, the smitten Captain impatiently waits for the sugars to be loaded and the cooperation of the Trade Winds to take him out to sea. Finally he is on his way only to be battled by fierce, winter storms as he sails from the warm tropical waters into the sleet laden winds of the north Atlantic. Undaunted, the Langley forges on as if it too has a mission that must not be denied. It is a happy day that the faithful brig again finds its mooring on the Sheerness sea wall.

It is no accident that she is at the Fountain Inn the day the Langley docks and it is not without purpose that William seeks a room for the night and the rest is history.

Time flies and the 15th of March, 1815 finds William back in Antigua alone under a full moon composing a love poem to Mary.

> *"Yes I heard the roaring ocean,*
> *whistling winds and beating rain,*
> *round me in convulsive motion,*
> *fierce my struggling canvas strain;*
> *wind and weather vied together,*
> *my poor vessel to subdue.,*
> *Tho' not regardless of the weather,*
> *all my soul was turned to you.*
> *Not a glimmering star to cheer me,*

thro' a dark and dismal night,
you alone were always near me,
image of celestial light.
Drenched by the bursting bellow,
watching how the tempest blew,
still I grasped the guide, my tiller,
hoped, and fondly thought of you.
Spread on down and angels waking
to protect an angel's form,
you perhaps each care foresaking,
scarcely heard the ruthless storm.
If you did, O say sincerely,
fiercer as the tempest grew,
did you think of one who dearly,
dearly loves to think of you?
William Byers
Langley, Spithead
March 13, 1815"

Captain William Byers

Captain William Byers was born in 1783 to Ann Nicholson Byers and William Byers, the sixth Captain Byers, of South Blyth, Northumberland, and later of Westoe, South Shields, County Durham, England. They named the boy William Nelson Edward. He was the second youngest of seven children.

Captain William Byers
(Original painting by Notman & Son,
Montreal, Byers family collection)

23

Thomas, the eldest son, was born in 1771 and died October 18, 1785. Sister Mary was born in 1767 and sister Elizabeth was born in 1773. The third sister, Dorothy, who married Captain Charles Thompson, was born April 10, 1775 and is very much a part of the story. James was born on October 16, 1778, and died on June 17, 1784. Charles, the youngest was born in April, 1789 and died in 1800.

The shared interest in the sea and the care of their elderly mother created a lasting bond between William and Dorothy and her family.

William's extended family were seafaring men, ship owners, co-partners, ship builders, merchants, dealers and chapmen. He was said to have been the "seventh of seven generations of Byers Sea Captains." He was a mariner, not just a sailor. The northeastern coast of England, especially the South Shields and Newcastle area, has always been the Byers home.

He grew up sailing with his father, learning the sugar, molasses and rum trade of the West Indies. To the plantation owners and other occupants on the islands they transported horses, asses and manufactured items from England. The women living so far from the London shops constantly needed things to enable the life style to which they were accustomed.

Captain William Sr. taught his son well, so that with his death in 1800, his son, at the age of 17, soon was able to step into his father's shoes. Mother and son vowed to go on. On the Brig Thomas, under the supervision and iron hand of Robert Thompson, Dorothy's brother-in-law, William carried on the traditions of his father. The affiliation with Robert Thompson was in the end a disappointing experience, one that plagued the finances of both mother and son for many years.

Ann and her son, William, operated as partners for some time. The Thomas was followed by the Langley. On February 17, 1807, Ann transferred her share of the Langley to her son so that at the age of 22 he was forging ahead creating a reputation and stories of his own.

> *"Be it remembered that I, Ann Byers, of Westoe, in the County of Durham, Widow, have this Day Sold and Transferred All my Right*

*Share, or interest of in, or to One full Moiety or Equal Half Part or
Share of and in the Ship Langley mentioned in the within
Certificate of Registry unto my Son, William Byers, of Westoe,
aforesaid in the County of Durham, Gentleman."*

In 1808, young William married his long time sweetheart, Ann
Stephenson. Before the marriage, she had given him a bit of a run around. On
one occasion when she wasn't around when he arrived home from a voyage,
he wrote, *"I am disappointed. I am sorry to find you so punctilious with me."*
The letter was never posted, but it was saved. Eventually, on May 8, in
Jarrow, Durham, England, Ann, the daughter of Captain and Mrs. George
Stephenson of South Shields, became his wife.

On March 4, 1809, Ann gave birth to a daughter, Elizabeth Stephenson
Byers, or "Eliza," as she was known for the rest of her life. The little family
planned to grow but it was not to be. Ann's second baby did not live, leaving
a grieving mother who, to ease her despondency, agreed to accompany her
husband on a voyage. Tragically, she became ill while at sea and died off the
coast of Spain. She is buried in Cadiz in Spain. William is devastated and
states that *"had it not been for the babe I would not have been able to go on."*
Little Eliza, with her father away at sea, is cared for by her two
Grandmothers, Byers and Stephenson, and her Aunt Dorothy Byers
Thompson.

It was in late summer or early autumn of 1814 that Captain William
returned to Sheerness and found the *"lady who had dreamed in the sun."*

The Courtship

William sweeps Mary off her feet. Her mother and Uncle William
Clarkson think that the Captain is moving much too quickly while at the
same time her two brothers are happy for their sister. James is married and
he and Miriam are expecting a baby and he wants the same happiness for his
sister.

Mary can no longer call her brother Ned a *"quack"*. He has finally completed his training as a surgeon/chemist, but now must find a suitable location to practice. Her bond with her two brothers is most important to her and she pledges to never break it when she has a family of her own. Little does she know how that bond will be stretched thin over the coming years.

In a classic case of do as I say not do as I do; Mary's friend, Catherine Fermore from Tusmore, tells her not to pay attention to her mother's reservations.

> *"I am glad you mentioned Captain Byers' affair (probably his first marriage), my uncle who is exactly of the same opinion as my father and thinks it to be the height of folly to either encounter Mrs. D's envious, sarcastic temper, or give credit to the report. No my love, let B. face her. He'll be able to defend himself. Therefore, do not let chat make you uncomfortable."*

Catherine Fermore, who is about to be married to Joseph Read, insists that her friend Mary be in attendance at the nuptial ceremony.

> *"I shall have more need of your consolation at this awful crisis than have yet ever had or shall have unless at the hour of my dissolution. What I regret most is my not being able to return your kindness in a similar occasion, whenever it may take place.*
>
> *I must beg another favour of you Mary, which is to get me a few things to bring down with you, namely a nice stylish dressing case, not as large as yours, but if you recollect, mine about that size. Don't exceed twelve shillings. My silk tassels, I think are too heavy so would thank you to bring me two white silk acorns. I shall want a hair brush to fit the case, and a comb, a bottle of lavender water, a night cap (don't laugh Mary), smart with edging of lace to it, and a muslin or whatever it is made of, to come round the head and tie. A little, not very little, white jarnet bag with tassels to it, which perhaps you would make on the occasion, but buy the cap I mind. A pair of gloves, yellow, last of all a dozen white cotton tufts for the front of my dressing gown. I request you to be particular in getting*

these articles to bring with you, as well as my bonnet. To prevent mistakes and trouble, have put them on a list."

With grace, good friend that she is, ladened with all that her fiend has requested and dresses in her best finery Mary returns to Tusmore determined to enjoy the wedding and all her friends, both family and staff. Her downstairs friends, she knows, will enjoy the stories of her holiday on the continent and sincerely wish her well as she embarks on a new life with William.

Mary and William 1815

In 1815, British law still decreed that one must be married by the Church of England in one's own community. To Mary's disappointment her Uncle William, a devout Roman Catholic, will not, or perhaps for safety sake, cannot attend. The wedding day finds him accompanying the wealthy Mrs. Willoughby, and enjoying the waters at Margate by the Sea.

And so it was that on August 30, 1815, at the Parish Church of St. George's in the East, London, the bells pealed out proclaiming the marriage of Captain William N.E. Byers and Mary Dudderidge.

The Honeymoon

Warm wishes from family and friends send them off on a two-part honeymoon. First, they must go north to South Shields, on the south side of the River Tyne to meet William's mother and Mary's new step-daughter, Eliza.

In a sweltering, crowded coach, *"they travel, most uncomfortably"* from London to York. An overnight stay allows them to visit the Cathedral, *"indeed a noble edifice and the principal object of attention in the city."* William does not find the coach ride very romantic and most emphatically says *"No more coach!"* Instead he hires a Post Chase to take them from Sunderland to Shields. The countryside is new to Mary and, like all tourists, she is glad that William takes her to see the much talked about Iron Bridge at Sunderland.

William's mother, Ann, warmly welcomes her new daughter-in-law and, thankfully, Mary and little Eliza bond instantly. The new mother has worried for nothing. In a letter to her mother, she says that *"the little girl cannot be seen without interesting your feelings, and appears to have an affectionate and amiable disposition."* Their love grows as they walk along the seaside cliffs and explore the area near Newcastle called Fenham, a place the extended Byers family has called "home" for generations.

Mary is the love of William's life and he worships the ground she walks on. She thinks that she must surely be dreaming; *"everything appears enchantment to me, but cannot last much longer."*

From the first of September to the last part of November Mary settles into her new life but still lives in her mother's home to ensure that little Eliza's move south will not cause her undue stress. She will be cared for by her new Grandmother Elizabeth while Mary embarks on the second leg of her honeymoon, a voyage to Antigua.

She has wished to sail and sail she will. With her brother James, for company and safety, she travels by stagecoach to Gravesend, a town on the south side of the Thames where the river meets the sea. On December 2, 1815, her brother leaves her with William on board the Brig Langley to await the winds that will carry them out to sea and on to Antigua, so far from family and home.

It all seems so easy and such fun to anchor for a night at the Nore sandbank in the estuary of the Thames. But one day does not a sailor make. Sea sickness, at its worst, is her companion on the second day. By dusk, able to eat *"the wings of a fowl"* she assures herself that she is not in *"a dying state."* Thankfully that is the end of her sickness and she is able to sail on enjoying the wind and the clean air.

The Captain's Mary

She is intrigued with the workings of the ropes and sails and becomes so helpful that years later William will say that *"he never had a first mate any better than his dear Mary."*

As she did while on the continent she faithfully writes to her mother. She begins with characterizing the very amusing crew. She is sure that she could furnish *"Hogarth the engraver of note at that time"* with many ideas for his work. The second mate, not too sure of himself, is much in awe of the Captain. The cook, with his loud voice and flying pots and pans, has very little consideration for anyone's quiet time. The steward, Mr. Dunn, who thinks himself a person of consequence, haughtily gives orders to his two helpers, poor, easily frightened Greenwich boys. One, a little slow, he calls *"Dozey"* and the other, *"a little brighter"*, is his assistant in the office of Steward. The groom, *"another droll"* jack-of-all-trades cleans the horses, scours the cabin, waits on table and pulls the ropes, etc., etc. They have all found out that the Captain has his limits. He will suffer no nonsense and has already dismissed a lad for being too saucy. He keeps them on their toes as he himself is *"everywhere in a minute"* and *"will remain stationary as long as a job lasts."*

Mary's admiration for the Captain knows no limits. She loves the billowing seas, the temperamental winds and the romance of the moon on the quiet midnight waters. There is nothing more beautiful than the reflection of the sunrise on the full blown sails and conquered waves. She vows to remember every magical moment for the rest of her life.

Madeira, a British Crown Colony since the Napoleonic Wars, is to be their first stop. *"After a week of beating about, the vessel almost touching the land, the wind still remaining contrary, we were obliged, to my infinite mortification, to turn our backs on the island, and make the best of a roundabout way, by the Canary Island to join the Trade Winds, but there was no choice in it. I can say nothing in their favour, for they were adverse all the time or nearly so."*

Finally, having battled constant storms, on December 17 they reach Madeira where William, out of necessity, leaves the ship and goes on shore.

After a short stay, *"at the peep of dawn"* he hails a boat and safely returns to the Langley vowing *"never to trust his dear self on the water again during the winter season."*

The weather will not cooperate and they are not able to weigh anchor but have to cut the cable and put to sea. The Captain did not wish, as others had, to be driven on shore during the night. With fair winds they come within sight of Porto Santo where once again the winds fail them.

Ships going south to the islands know that adding wine and lace to their cargo always ensures certain easy profit. Mary wishes she had been able to see the much heralded resorts, similar to Margate and other English southeastern coastal retreats which the wealthy from the continent have built on the island.

Christmas at sea is lonely but helped by Mary reliving, in her imagination, her traditions at home. She assures her mother that Byers *"is most kind and attentive"* and that he sends *"all good wishes to the Cockneys. You cannot tell how much I thought of you at Christmas time and if it pleases God, I look forward to it with something more than pleasure to permit us all to meet once again. We shall enjoy the happiness of each other's society with double zest from this separation."*

Finally land is in sight; it had been a long time at sea for a beginner!

Antigua 1816

"Without having suffered any material injury from their aforesaid boisterous passage" on January 20, 1816, the Langley safely reaches Parham, Antigua. It was a long voyage and it is a long way from home. In years to come the experience of this first voyage will help her to weather, time after time, the many lonely months when William is away.

Antigua is, at this time, the gateway to the Caribbean. The sugar era began when the British settled the island in 1632 and, as a British colony, it became another spot favored by the merchant classes. Antigua benefited from their money as families moved in and created large sugar plantations which prospered until 1834 when slavery was abolished. Securing a shipload of sugar, molasses and rum was often tedious and discouraging business. Waiting times were too often long, especially when dull winds delayed the workings of the sugar mills.

Vessel repair on this island was made easier by Admiral Horatio Nelson's building of a dock yard in 1784 at English harbour in Antigua. British naval facilities were developed and shipping laws were strengthened.

Although this was of great benefit to the island Nelson was not well received by the locals. *"The vile natives"* would not allow him to live on shore. His home was his ship.

Thankfully William is much respected and no such obstacles are ever in his way.

Mary immediately falls in love with the beauty of the island and the warm waters of the sea. She cannot wait to explore it and that is just what she and William do as soon as the Langley is moored in Parham Harbour and the Captain's orders to his crew have been made clear.

Mary writes to her mother. *"Parham is a very retired, pleasant place, which suits me. 'Tis the most healthy spot on the island. We have a pleasant house by the seaside with the ship in view of it. It consists of two sitting and two bed rooms, surrounded by coconut trees, and we have a flag staff for a signal when a boat is needed from the ship."* It is just too beautiful and romantic to be true. They can come and go as they wish. Their wish is their command.

Immediately they are welcomed into the social life of the plantation owners. They visit Mrs. Ottley, *"a very sensible, pleasant woman with a charming family of children"* and they dine with Mrs. Rogers whose grown up daughter will be company for Mary. Mrs. Ottley and Mrs. Rogers, the wives of plantation owners, welcome Mary with gifts of fruit and milk. These two women will be part of Mary's life until 1833.

Some places are real eye-openers. St. Johns is *"a noisy bustling place not at all to my taste."* Mary is amused at the *"air of consequence and the dresses of the negroes that were as fine as hands could make."* She is *"distressed and offended at the scarce clothing of the slaves, scarce enough to cover their nakedness. Is shocking to humanity, tho' I am told many of them are happy and do not feel the misery we so much commiserate."* She is heartened to learn that they are much better off than years before and that the children are well cared for. Mary again soon decides that Parham is the *"healthiest spot on the island."*

They had brought horses to Antigua and thankfully the animals weathered the trials of the voyage very well. Byers sells some but keeps a mare for himself and a pony for Mary so that they can ride together. The days are of equal length all year round and darkness sets in at six in the evening. Clear as day, moonlight evenings provide many romantic rides and sojourns on the beach.

Letters from Mary's mother assure her that little Eliza is doing well even though she seems to be subject *"to an attack that will return if not attended to."* She cautions her mother to *"not keep her too close to school but to let her go, read and say her lessons and come home frequently."*

She continues, *"The crops are plentiful but late and they will probably not be able to leave for home before May."* She tells the story of two of the Captain's sailors who are in trouble. One is in prison and one has run away. Byers and a gentleman armed with a great stone in a handkerchief and an unloaded pistol hunted them down in a field of cane.

She assures her Mother that she is very happy and that the climate agrees with her. *"Life here is much easier to live than in London except for the mosquitoes"* who are eating her alive and leaving her looking as if she has small pox. These back and forth letters keep loneliness at bay.

On a five day trip to Barbuda, a nearby island surrounded by reefs and rocks, Byers joins a hunting party. This flat island, where no sugar can be grown, is used to breed oxen, sheep, goats, horses, and mules that are hunted when needed. She spends a nervous time waiting. She has been told that the hunt can be dangerous if a bull, singled out, is *"one of the fiercest among them."* Thankfully, Byers had a good time and no mishap marred the adventure.

The next day, April 26, 1816, back in Parham, Mary must hurry. She must tell her mother about the hunt. The West Indian, with Captain Cook, is sailing tomorrow and her letter must go with his leaving.

Finally, after receiving only three letters in five months, a letter dated January 28, 1816, arrives. There is good news and bad. James and Miriam have a baby son. Eliza, although still deaf, is improving. Edward's letter tells that the Fountain Inn is in trouble. George Clarkson, Elizabeth's brother, has died and the inn must be sold. Mrs. Clarkson has until Christmas to sell and move her family to Gloucestershire. Hopefully they will be able to survive by starting a dressmaking business. Mary, for the first time, wishes she is not so far from home.

Time passes. Visits with the Ottley's, the Rogers' and the Watson's are always welcome. The horses and cargo that they brought to Antigua have been sold giving the Captain a good profit.

News of desperate living conditions in London has reached them. *"Only three pounds of coal a day allowed for each house."* It has been easy for a while to forget some of these hardships.

All good things must come to an end. They must leave their paradise island and return to the real world. In February they start to load the sugars; it won't be long now and they will be on their way. Thankfully they will go home with a full load.

A letter, dated August 11, 1816, from the Captain, in South Shields, to Mary, in London, reveals that they have arrived home safely by mid-summer.

A Home and a Family

The honeymoon is over and Mary begins to chart the road she will travel for the next seventeen years of her life. She is tanned and healthy and anxious to establish their new home. William, on the other hand, after leaving some of his cargo at Sheerness, has taken the remaining sugar, etc. north to the South Shields area. Here he will load with coal to bring back and sell in the London.

It does not take long to get into the swing of things and she knows that she will have to resign herself to being on her own a great deal. When apart they write faithfully, sometimes daily. The mail depends on whatever ship is sailing and however long the voyage takes, sometimes causing multiple letters to arrive on the same day.

A letter from South Shields, dated August 11, 1816, tells us that Ned Dudderidge is with William in hopes that he will be able to join Dr. Trotter's medical practice in Newcastle. This was not to be, as *"even doctors complain - them leaches - it appears as if poverty made the masses healthful."* He has not been able to establish himself in the London area and reluctantly agrees to sail with Captain William to Antigua in hopes that he might be needed there.

Meanwhile, the wait for coals is long. William is very lonesome and Ned is crabby. William writes, *"Ah, my sweet girl that sand that arm and arm we walked over as light and pleasantly as if it had been one of Nature's carpets, assisted by love, that lightens and brightens every scene, Ned grumbles at. I am impatient to join you again. Shields has very few charms for me."*

Ned, seldom out of the city, cannot help wondering that places and things are not like London. Walking over the sands in the morning annoys him and he often explains. *"Can we not have a boat in the river Byers?"* The two may have a difficult time together on the long voyage to the Islands.

William's mother, Eliza's main caregiver, misses the little girl but knows that she must return to London to her new mother. It is time to change her own life and she agrees to live with her daughter, Dorothy, and to send her furniture to London for her son's new home. She knows that she cannot change the course of time.

Meanwhile Mary has found that her mother, having lost her position at the Fountain Inn and upset with the idea of her daughter leaving her home, has disappeared to the baths at Margate. Mary copes on her own, sorting her belongings, searching for a place and finally moves to 102 Hammet Street, Minories, London. She must be ready for the arrival of little Eliza.

The years to come will fall into a pattern. William's letters will convey good news and bad. She will celebrate the good and bolster him through the bad. She will manage their finances and survive through London's troubled times. Love, courage and determination will help her to face the challenge of raising her family. She is happy and content, confident that dreams do come true.

William has been most truthful concerning business troubles he and his mother have had in the past. Mary knows that they have suffered losses due to something Dorothy's brother-in-law Robert Thompson had caused to be done and is concerned when he tells her, "*Robert Thompson, I shall see tomorrow. You may depend on me being calm. I have too good a hold on him to commit myself by rashness.*" This is an old argument and needs to be resolved as soon as possible if family harmony is to be maintained.

William's sister, Dorothy, has finally seen the light. She had been dubious as to Mary's ability to properly raise little Eliza and has had the nerve to suggest that Mary "*keep her Betsey*" for a year. William quips "*I am glad my sister has at length opened her eyes. When she comes to town you can talk about it.*"

This is mostly good news but the indignant new mother sincerely hopes she will encounter no cumbersome in-law interference.

Mary's Roman Catholic faith, so precarious in Protestant England, prompts a word of warning from William. "*My dear Mary, let me caution you to take care of your sweet self. I did not like to see you had been at Chapel with*

Mother." He understands her faith but he doesn't want her in the middle of a religious argument.

Life settles down giving them only about a month of family time together before William leaves for Antigua. Life is good and he leaves knowing that a loving bond has formed between his wife and daughter.

Voyages and Letters

November 6, 1816, finds William on the Langley, off the coast of Kent, going into the Downs, an area of the southern North Sea, near the English Channel. It is the first challenge of getting out to sea. Bordered by the white Cliffs of Dover, storms, from any direction, can drive ships onto shore or onto the shifting sands.

A short letter offers the security any new wife needs. *"We have been so busily employed that neither Ned nor me have seen our faces till we shaved this moment. Perhaps it is as well, for the reflection would only be a misery. The confusion of last voyage is nothing to this. It requires all my head to put all to rights. Mr. Grewcock won't stay tonight, and I don't like to lose any chance of writing to my darling, hoping she is well."*

November 14, in spite *"of seas stronger than usual"* they are anchored at Motherbank, a shallow sand bar off the northeast coast of the Isle of Wight. He had been on shore but the *"size of the tavern bill"* prompted him to hire a waterman to take him back to the brig. The high swells have made him unexpectedly uneasy. He has weathered worse but, on account of Mary, his life seems clearer. He must get to Antigua and back to his family as quickly as he can.

> *"I find things onboard the ship tolerable. I am certain King would make a better Master than a Mate. I have had all our hay and corn overhauled, and find the expenditure has been too much, and think, if the wind doesn't come fair, soon must have to buy more. The man certainly labours under a disadvantage, by the hay being so near the beasts, but still the want of thought and care is plain*

enough. Too many people can do well enough in the common truck of life, but should they be pushed out of the direct line, become helpless as babes."

The wind does not let up making it necessary to buy more beef and rations. Knowing Mary expects some money he promises to send £10 while on shore, or if not, by the Monday Post. Being married hasn't changed the fact that money is always a problem.

Mary shivers as she reads. *"The wind is now blowing as it did that day in the Sound last year, very cold at NNW with flying snow showers. The land is covered with snow, and I expect the wind to easterly every hour."* If he had known the winds would be so troublesome he would not have set out so soon.

They had parted in good spirits leaving him an easy mind. *"A sailor's is a hard life for both parties, but still, my dear girl, the hope of return takes the sting from adieu, and when together, no people live so happy."*

It is late in the season with stormy seas and cold northwest squalls. Ice and snow freeze their hands to the ropes and *"set fear in their hearts."* Ned is useless as a sailor and Mary chuckles to learn that her Captain says that *"He is more woman than his sister. She is a better sailor than any gentleman who ever swam salt water with me."* Even though they are off to a bad start, *"the horses are hearty, the puppies and the rest of the horses and livestock are well but one of the asses has died."*

The winds did moderate. *"This morning found the wind at ESE, which is very good while it lasts, which is seldom long. A few days and then a NW won't hurt us. This is a lottery and blank or prize, I must draw it."*

Sixteen days after leaving home, *"the pilot takes them out to sea."* The Captain proudly boasts that the *"old Brig behaved like a sea fowl – last breeze in the short sea - there she surprised me how dry she went."*

On they go battling the northern clime until at last the winds bring warmth, the skies are higher, the water less troubled and spirits improve.

1817

January the 2ⁿᵈ, two months after leaving home the Langley arrives safely in Antigua. *"We arrived here, I mean Parham, the day after New Year's Day."* The long wait for the sugars will vary very little from previous trips except that Ned's company will be a welcome diversion.

> *"Ned, I am happy to say pleases me much, which already shows the*
> *good effects of his being without his mother's immediate support.*
> *We have agreed better than could have been expected from two*
> *such opposite tempers."*

The winter is most difficult for both William and Mary. Mary is pregnant and William is obsessively fearful that he might lose her. There are mobs in the streets of London and he *"trusts that she will not know any more disturbance from them. A fright might be very dangerous to you."* Mary, at home, preparing for her baby, has her mother for comfort and advice. Ned, being too young to confide in, leaves William alone with his fears. Memories of the death of his first wife, Ann, haunt him.

William's own words, January 24ᵗʰ, convey just how difficult his life is.

> *"Indeed, my love, I am so tired of the voyage, that I do not know*
> *how I exist. Fancy oft wafts me home, where I enjoy in ideas the*
> *converse of my dear Mary. Life is short and hard. It is that so*
> *much of it should be spent far, far from all that makes it valuable.*
> *Two or three months might be born but more is too much. If I must*
> *go to sea all my life, let it be in a trade where I can be more at*
> *home with my family. However these hard times continue, my love,*
> *we must be content to live any way that is honest."*

There are always troubles with at least one of the crew and this group is no exception.

> *"Jim Kearns still continues very ill. He has tried to run away*
> *through the means of Mr. Charles Wood, who assisted him in*
> *getting all his new clothes on shore. We neglected your advice,*
> *thinking the fellow would not think of going away 'til cured. I wrote*

*Wood yesterday that if things were not sent onboard today, I would
resort to other methods. There is gratitude. He also behaved very
insolent on the passage, and took himself forward, but the people,
being on allowance, then tired of entertaining him. So, after a
struggle between his hunger and pride, he entreated to be admitted
into the steerage again. His brother has been nearly dead with
fever. You would laugh to hear him tell us how he got it. It's a
custom with the slaves the night that begins the holidays, after
midnight, to so muster all the music they can and dance about the
estate. It seems Mr. Wood was not appraised of this, when he heard
the noise of a drum and a fiddle, he jumped out the window, and
ran 'till he dropped, and was found insensible. We think he must
have been praying his devotions that night, I won't say to Bacchus,
but the humble God, whoever he is, of New Rum. He's not married,
but says he would marry her daughter, who he called a damned
fine girl."*

Money has become an issue with an island family, his friends, the Allans.
Mrs. Allan has made a fuss about the bill for goods William brought her from
London so that now William does not feel that he should accept an invitation
for dinner. On board, in Parham Harbour, William chastises Mary for asking
him to kiss the Allan children for her. *"Indeed Mary, you must have forgot
how much I dislike to kiss any but my own. It appears we are to have three
beside our dear Elizabeth. At least I have several times dreamed so, even
last night."*

The Mail Packet is two days late at Barbados. With no recent news from
Mary, a *"heartily tired,"* lonesome William writes this poem, February 14th,
1817.

> *"I've wandered east and west.*
> *Pleasure in every clime I found,*
> *But sought, in vain, for rest*
> *While glory sighs for other spheres.*
> *I feel that one too wide,*
> *And think the home which love endears*
> *Were worth the world beside."*

Mary is not having an easy pregnancy, prompting William to say. *"I am sorry, my love, you are any worse than when I left you. I thought the worst symptoms were past. I wish to God I was with you to keep your spirits up. However, my dear, you don't want resolution in a good cause, and to them, God and your Mother's care, I commit you. I charge you, Mary, not to risk getting cold by getting up too soon."*

It is amusing that William has been reading Ned's medical book and sees it as very dangerous. *"I think you told me you intended dipping the dear infant in cold water. It must be a good thing, only minding at first to suit the coldness of the water to the strength of the child. It stands to reason that at first a weakly child cannot stand the shock of cold as well as a strong one, tho' by properly preparing the weak child, to bear the cold by beginning with the chill of the water at first it will, in the end, receive the most benefit. I have a shower bath every morning and find myself as well as can be in any climate."*

William continues to relay his loneliness and fears in a letter dated the 20th.

> *"My darling, I am all hopes and fears, and anxiety. The latter part of February and the beginning of March now fast approaches. Would to God I was with you! Happy, happy, our ancestors have been before they were discovered by the Romans, when content with their native land, neither lure nor ambition tempted them to cross the seas. Then, after their day's hunt their evenings were spent with their wives and children. Their wants were few and easy supplied. Now men, thanks to the refinements we have at last assured at, must go long voyages, cross seas, and run also the risk of unhealthy climates, and only to obtain a scanty subsistence in this world of care and strife. Remove three or four people out of it and I am sure I could die with pleasure at home. I am distracted with my money concerns and already with wishing myself at home. I hope, my love, your time will not run so far as the first Wednesday of March. There is every chance of my being here long enough to receive letters by that Packet. Oh Mary, it harrows my blood to think you might not be alive to read this. I have so constantly lost*

my dearest affections that it makes me dread the risk your precious life runs."

Letters like this are not very uplifting especially when there is no expected money in the envelope. Money will be a challenge over the years and sometimes the cause of marital stress.

Wheeling and dealing and dreaming are a big part of William's life because the West Indies' trade alone gives little hope of making security to retire.

William's of April 20, 1817, gives Mary some reason to think that things are looking up, but really she knows it is too good to be true. A merchant wants to charter the Langley to go from London to America to load lumber to bring back to Antigua. The money, £720 to £800, sounds good but the idea of buying another vessel of 200 tons, (if Mother will give part of Sheerness money) and sharing profits with others instantly waves a red flag in her mind. William believes that in five years he would be able to retire. *"I am equal to it, and I know, my dear Mary, will be as much with me as possible. Indeed, I would not think of it if I did not know my girl was a good sailor and would go round the world with me, so make up your mind to see Yankey Land."*

It was too good to be true. All around the *"nation is brought to a pretty pitch, hard times abound."* William is having a hard time getting promised sugars. Late, sparse crops cause plantation owners to renege on what has been promised to each waiting vessel. Ned's skills are not needed on the Island and at home James is doing very little business.

All of this prompts William to say, *"I shall soon be ready to say I am a Yankey, for now there is neither honour nor profit in being an Englishman. I don't know a man who has less ties to reconcile him to live in the now poor world."* He goes on to tell Mary that she need not worry about having great worldly goods. *"Indeed Mary, I am afraid that will never come to pass, and 'till it does, we will, I am certain, be as happy as most of the people. It luckily happens neither of us expects or wishes for much. Thank God our minds are pretty congenial."*

William attends a party on Long Island, near Parham, where there are several ladies who cannot compare to his Mary, *"one was too fair, the other too brown."* Always lonesome, he says he cannot see any lady that *"looks like my Mary in her face"* and that the *"old Langley jacket shall be tight laced the passage home."* Five months is a long time to wait for the sugars and be away from his wife.

William wishes for a son to name Nelson but sometime after March 19th Mary successfully delivers a wee daughter and calls her Mary. "The *wee lass will be so comfortable in the skin lined with silk that Miss Roger has made for her dear friend's new baby."*

Finally, after a wait of five months, June 9th, the Langley sails for home. William, knowing his *"money affairs are not pleasant,"* hopes that Mary will see the villainy of others and just be glad to have him home to bond with their new daughter.

In a letter, never mailed, he pours out his loneliness. Poor health and depression are his constant companions. Mary never reads this one but others carry a similar message so that she has to digest and lock it all away so that she may keep her spirits up and create a happy home for her children. Sometimes it is not easy.

Langley at Sea, June 15th, 1817

"I could not sleep the last night, for the thoughts of sailing in the morning, or the next two nights. However, my mind is now more tranquil. I can now close out the night, but hardly does it deserve the name of sleep. Your miniature hangs by my bed foot. It's the last thing I look at, at night, and first thing in the morning. I have actually persuaded myself it's a likeness.

So much for absence. However, in this life there's an alloy to every happiness. Knowing I shall find my money affairs unpleasant - perhaps I anticipate them worse than I shall find them - throws a damp over my mind, yet why shall despair? I know my dear Mary is willing to share my lot and will never reproach me with what the villainy of others, and the sudden change of times have brought about. As it is, I think to be done with the Langley may be one of the best things I ever met with.

My time is only bruised, and when left to my own exertions, must then put forth my whole strength, which little as it is, has brought me through scenes of danger and difficulty where the biggest has lain down. My Antigua connection will always procure me friends, and my dear father was older than me when Providence put him into the anyway of making what I have been robbed of. Yet my dear Mary, it requires all my fortitude to think of giving up, not only what my father left us, but what I have worked for myself these last ten years. What unhappiness it has caused my poor Mother. It alone must be a heavy charge against Robert Thompson, to abuse her goodness in the way he has done.

Had I not the tender ties I have to confine me to England, I should set out for South America and there, either make a name and fortune, or die in helping to throw off the yoke of Spanish Tyranny, and God knows, without my Mary, my Elizabeth, and I trust another sweet babe, and my mother, sister and brothers, life would be a wide blank and glad should I be to lay it down, my love. I am not in a desponding humour at this moment. It's my settled thoughts, for had I not had my Elizabeth at her mother's death, I should have followed her in a little time, owing to the weak state I was in, but the sight of my helpless child seemed to brace every nerve, and, I trust I have always performed a parent's part towards her, tho' in examining my own heart, I think I don't love her with a love I see some do their children, neither did I think I did her Mother, or do I you, my love, or my mother. I believe I have told you so before. I trust I am wrong, for God knows I feel enough for you all. Am not only thankful to God for the dear wife he has given me but also for her mother, as another parent, for very soon I may be deprived of my own, and should also my Mary go, I should be without her, without an advisor or monitor to direct my frail bark over the ocean of despair? I have made my mind up, dear wife - you have had a safe delivery, on that point my mind is firm."

The Trade Winds are causing the Brig to make poor progress, but with all studdensails set the Captain hopes for a strong and fair gale that will help make up some time.

William goes on.

> *"Thank God, he's made both our minds humble. We have no ambitious view to torment us. The most we ever wished for was enough to keep me at home, and if that wish is withheld from us, I agree with my love, it's for some wise end of Providence.*
>
> *If we look around us, we'll not see any family that has not had something to disturb them, and whilst we are happy in mutual love and esteem - I say esteem - for we may love an object that is a constant source of uneasiness to us, and have enough to keep the wolf from the door, our chance of happiness is small. Many others - the times have hurt - who are past meridian of life and unable to work."*

November 6th, 1816, the Langley had been *"going into the Downs"* on its way to Antigua, now eight months later, July 17th, 1817, it is again *"at the Downs on its way home."*

The Captain and the Langley had made their last voyage. Mary posts its sale at the Lloyd's Coffee House and hopes that it sells quickly.

FOR SALE

At Lloyd's Coffee-House,

On THURSDAY the 26th day of MARCH, 1818,

THE BRIG

LANGLY,

254½ Tons, per Register,

Now lying on the South Side of the West India Export Dock.

INVENTORY.

Hull, Masts, Yards, Standing and Running Rigging, with all Faults as they now lie.

Anchors.	Carpenter & Boatswain's Stores.	1 Ditto heel tackle blocks
2 Best bowers		1 Set of lumber irons
1 Small ditto	1 Spare lower yard	3 Crow bars
1 Large kedge	1 Ditto topmast	2 Pair boat's lashings
1 Small ditto	1 Ditto span	2 Pitch pots
1 Boat's anchor	6 Oak planks	1 Half watch tackle
Cables.	2 Skids	1 Jigger
2 Bower cables	6 Steering sail booms	2 Cat head stoppers
1 Stream ditto	18 handspikes	2 Shank painters
1 Warp	6 Capstern bars	6 Spare dead eyes
1 Sea buoy rope	4 Oars	2 Serving mallets
1 Nun buoy	2 Boat's davits	Ship Chandler's Stores.
Sails.	3 Pair of screws	2 Three pound guns and
2 Jibs	1 Grindstone	overalshot
2 Fore topmast staysails	2 Pump brake	1 Deep sea lead and line
2 Foresails	4 Spare boxes	1 Hand ditto
3 Topsails	2 Lower ditto	4 Ballast shovels
2 Top gallant sails	4 Pump boits	1 Ensign, jack and pendant
2 Royals	2 Ditto houle	1 Horn lanthorn
1 Square mainsail	6 Hatch bars	1 Pair steelyards
2 Fore and after ditto	3 Ditto tarpaulins	3 Oil bottles
1 Main staysail	2 Scrubbing brushes	6 Padlocks
1 Main topmast ditto	1 Long tar ditto	1 Cook's hearth
2 Lower steering sails	1 Short ditto	1 Cabin stove
3 Topmast ditto	5 Pair can hooks	2 Hen coops
2 Top gallant ditto	4 Marline spike	6 Anchor stock hoops
2 Bundles of boat sails	4 Scrapers	A quantity of old staves and
1 Awning and some old canvas	1 Cat block	fire wood.
	1 Set of purchase blocks and fall	Boats.
	1 Ditto top ditto	2 Boats at Mr. Foster's, boat Builder

The Brig and Stores to be taken with all faults as they now lie, without any allowance for length, weight, quantity or quality, or any defect whatever. Inventories may be had on Board, and of

R. & R. BROWN,

30, St. MARY HILL.

Peter Skipper and Son, Printers and Stationers, Mincing Lane.

Sale of the Langley
(Original document, Byers family collection)

The Neptune 1817 and 1818

Economic pressures do not allow William to tarry long with his family. No special Christmas again for him. December 18th, 1817, on his new brig, the Neptune, he is heading south midst blistering cold and *"severe gales."* Anchored at the Nose, waiting for favourable winds to allow the pilot to tow them out to sea, with cold cramped fingers, he writes to his mother. She is failing and he hopes that she will see the winter through.

Strapped for money, once more, with only £5 and a monthly note to send back home he stresses that Mary must get after Charles Thompson for the £500 he owes them. On a positive note he ends by saying that *"the Neptune seems in better plight than I thought her."*

In 1817 Mary's address had changed from 102, Hammet, Minories, to No. 3 Ireland's Row, London. Now in 1818 she lives at 105 Minories for a time and then the letters are sent to 127 Fenchurch Street, London. Considering that Mary is pregnant again and caring for wee Mary these moves present great difficulty for the young woman but she never seems to complain and patiently waits for more letters.

January 3, 1818, the Neptune is at sea three days sail southward of Madeira,

> *"having had winds from the Downs that were fair and blowed*
> *fresh. A fresh gale and a strange ship found me plenty of*
> *employment. Indeed, my love, so awkward were things that I am*
> *sure the Langley was easier worked with half the hands. A*
> *continuance of bad weather left me little time for reflection. Every*
> *hour was employed, not in making alterations, but improvements,*
> *and with very scanty means. However, luckily my predecessors had*
> *found means to get many articles of pride, which I have converted*
> *into articles of real use at no expense. She is now made handy to*
> *me. I find many causes to miss the old brig, except the Neptune*
> *steers better. There is no other way to compare the Langley, who*
> *would carry less sail, when the other must lay too or wash*
> *everything off her decks. I gave her one trial and found her as wet*

as a deep loaded vessel, but when I took the sail off her and laid
her too, she made very good weather. However, she is tight. I must
not, indeed, expect to find many ships like the Langley who would
certainly roll before the wind but keep her nose to it. She would
live like a duck."

After a cold stormy start the voyage is a comfortable one except for a blow to William's thigh. *"A block of lightning as big as a full moon"* caused a block strap to fall on his leg. He heartily damns the ship and all concerned and after limping around for a few days is fully recovered. *"My luck is not the best in the world, (but) it always stops short of great ills."*

All painted and shined, the Neptune safely reaches Parham, Antigua, January 18th, 1818. The crops are good and give promise of a full load. The Captain is in good spirits but he does have one worry. He thinks that he has left Mary in the family way again and is *"vexed"* with himself for letting it happen. He says that the heyday of his life is past, that it is love not desire that impels his soul to her. (Little does he know that in twelve years she will give birth six times.) Regardless of the tiffs Mary has sent with him a pair of her new drawers and because he is lonely he puts them on and says *"I will wear them as long as they last."*

Friends on the island ask warmly for Mary prompting William to urge her to plan to travel with him on the next voyage.

He apologizes for the *"little broils"* that marred his last stay at home.

"It's true I tend to view things with that vivid eye. I did, but
seldom, look back with regret to the fire I have seemed to let
disturb a tranquility I did not before possess and look back to the
past as a fearful dream, when with passions as unrestrained as
wild colts, I drove before the game. But till honour, whilst passions
held madly the sway, still kept watch in my tumult tossed soul, and
my dearest Mary is the beacon that has steered me into, I trust, the
Harbour of Love."

She enjoys news that is worth future debate. Danger and excitement capture her interest.

"About three weeks ago, three South American Man-of-War commanded by Admiral Biron appeared in St. Johns. I went on board them with Mr. Hornell. Two were loaded with mules for sale. They had every appearance of poverty, their crews composed of all nations, even Indians. The Governor would not let them anchor, owing to them being armed vessels. He said they came straight from the River Oronokee, sent to raise money for their government, but the opinion here is that they had plundered some town belonging to the Royalists. One of the brig's captains was an Englishman with trousers on with British Lieutenant's buttons. No doubt that he is one. He said he had only been out a few months. They had not a watch on board. They represented their cause in a flourishing way, but were themselves poor specimens of it."

More news for debate, but this debate Mary vows to win.

He has read one of Mary Woolscanscraft's books called *"The Rights of Women"* and gives her his opinion.

"I agree with her in many things but she doesn't know when to stop. A woman of sense may read it but it would upset a girl. We better take the world as it is, than by broaching new and strange opinions make it worse. I agree with her that the wife should be the friend of the husband, that the union should be founded on mutual esteem. She lays a great stress on enjoyment palling in possession, and then if there is no esteem, love is gone etc. etc. Well grant it is. A man then begins to look more into his wife's qualities and should he find, as has been my own happy case, more reason to admire and esteem her every day, it's all right. But should a wife want a voice in parliament, neglect my babies in studying politics, and consider she had the same cards to play in the world as myself, I should d--n all her great sense, and wish she had no more than to know than how to make me a new shirt, be a kind mother to my children and a dutiful wife to myself. I shall try to recollect what more she says. It will help to pass an hour away when we have the happiness of chatting together. Her own conduct and pupils have been far from exemplary."

The news that one of the horses taken to Antigua has died and that action is being taken against the ship, with a trial set for May the fifth, is very worrying. Hopefully, the fact that the new owner, Mr. Wyke, is known to whip his animals will bring a verdict in the ship's favour. William quips; *"my poor Father seems to have taken all the family luck with him, and left me to struggle with rascals."*

Months go by with no letters, no news from home, spirits fall aided by again promises of loading not kept. Then all at once weeks of letters arrive. All are relieved that Ned is settled in Fenchurch Street with hopes of success. The fact that there is no mention of the sale of the Langley is worrisome. He had hoped that Mary would have had the much needed money by now.

By mid-February Mary is weighed down with illness and fatigue. She is pregnant and little Mary is very ill. *"My love, even what we call our blessings, bring its troubles with it. However, as these things are the common lot of humanity, we must even bear them, trusting should the dear little soul live to be a woman, that she will afford us more comfort than trouble, which in anything is as much as can be looked for in this world."*

Mary wishes for shorter voyages and mentions the coal trade that would keep him closer to home. He assures his exhausted wife that employment in the coal trade is also his fervent wish but says. *"Whatever we shall consider most conducive to our family interest shall be our guide."* Even with all this *"they are both thankful for the good and thank God that the bad is not worse."*

William reflects on his life.

> *"I have been reviewing my past life since my boyhood. Alas, alas, how little to be pleased with except the conscious satisfaction of never wronging a fellow creature, nor doing a dishonourable action. Had I met with common fair play in the world, how different would my circumstances have been this day? My poor father seems to have taken all the family luck with him, and left me to struggle with rascals, with a heart too open to suspect, and at too great a distance to prevent the ruin of the family. When I*

consider the act of Robert Thompson and the gradual way he brought it about, I cannot blame my poor mother. It's no use to look back, but to mend the future by it. It has proved a clear lesson, but the very value of it must make me attend the more to it, in my future intercourse with the world. Although I have had a good share of trouble in my time, let us hope, my love, the worst is past. As an individual, it could not fret me, but as a husband and a father, it makes me wince, when I think about it. There is only one bright shade in the picture and that's my dear Mary. Blessed with you, many other things bear lightly on my troubled feelings. Perhaps it might have been better for you had you never known such a luckless Wight. But you would never get a man who pleases more than yourself, and as you are not as anxious of wealth, I don't doubt but we will live as happy a life as falls to the lot of most mortals."

He does provide a chuckle to lighten the mood a bit. It worked and brought a blush to his wife's cheeks. *"I was told a story that made me smile yesterday. Indeed I cannot get it out of my mind. It appears that night, my love, we slept at Anthony Wykes', and that Mrs. W. was awoke by a noise which she thought was a cat among her china. She called her maid to see what it was - who told her it was only the Capt. and his wife."*

May 2nd finds William still in Parham hoping that when he gets home he will find his *"little Mary running alone."* He believes that the wee girl is made of good stuff and when once she gets over her weaning and measles she will get strong.

Finally, by the end of May, the Neptune is loaded with three hundred hogsheads of sugar, all the rum it can store and for Mary a small black terrier and a goat for milk for little Mary. July 31, 1818, the Captain, in view of the white chalk cliffs of Dover, is on his way home to his three girls.

Mary is happy that William is serious about not wanting to sail south again but is disappointed when a meeting with his cousin Michael Byers, just back from Archangel, Russia, does not end in William's favour. Michael's brig, the Bridgett, a very different vessel than the Neptune, is a coppered ship with *"everything as it ought to be on the Master's part"* but there is none available at this time for William. There are two vessels for sale in London, so if he has no luck in Newcastle or Sunderland he will try his luck in London on his way home.

Thankfully luck is on his side, not only in seeking a vessel suitable for the coal trade but most importantly in the fact that he spends a warm Christmas and New Years with his family. With Mary exhausted and wee Mary weakened and failing he dreads having to leave and head out for Antigua again.

1819

January, 1819, Mary has another brig to sell. Having spent time in Shields, William has bought the very much lauded ship, Antaeus. *"A stronger vessel never was built, and with the advantage of having every good property. I am afraid I shall get too fond of her. It's so many years since I was at sea in a fine ship."*

The winter months slip away with the business part of Mary's life being easier in that William has been able to borrow £3800 and arrange partnerships through Mr. Swanson negating the need to use her mother's money. He even remembers to pay his fees to the *"Master Mariners"* before leaving for Antigua. Still the shadow over the house lingers on, good days and bad. Love, doctoring and prayers seem in vain.

As feared the unspeakable happens! July 3, 1819 little Mary passes away. In a letter of that date, from Edward, William learns the tragic news. Once again he curses the distance from home. Antigua is just too far from Mary.

> *"My Dear Mary,*
>
> *I have just received Edward's kind but sad letter. My love, all my feelings on the occasion are for you. I have inured myself to think the dear little thing would not be long spared us makes me feel it less, but your last letter revived my slender hope. You said the Dear*

had got so much stronger and the season of the year being so favourable. Alas, we are certain of nothing in this world. Just when we begin to hope the best, the worst takes place. Edward assures me that your health is good and that you bear it heroically. That my darling is like yourself, but still I would feel more assured had you wrote me yourself. Yet, the sad task is better spared you. This world is but at best a place of trial. The dispensation of God, I always cheerfully bow my head to. And you Mary, with a strong, firm mind and a large share of religion, I hope will not let your tenderness get the better of your fortitude. No, I know, my Mary, for my sake, will not let her spirits droop under it, as well as for the infant unborn, who I trust will be blessed with better health, and live to repay us for the loss of poor Mary."

Heavy with child, Mary, with the help of her mother, somehow gets herself strong again. She has a new baby to bring into the world; she has no choice.

September the fourth, at the Downs, nearly home, just one month after the death of little Mary, a relieved father learns that, August 21st his wife has safely delivered a healthy baby boy, William Edward Nelson. Again he is just too long away from his family.

The autumn brings some well-earned family time but the Captain must sail again. Once again, Christmas Eve, off St. Michael's, Western Islands, off the coast of Portugal the winds have finally stilled and he writes to his *"Dear Mary."*

It hadn't been a very good beginning, just too much fierce wind and weather. *"The sailors are much in need of land having weathered, not too successfully, terrible south to southwest gales."* Rough seas cause animals to go down. Kicking asses and horses, on top of each other, results in the death of nine asses and two horses. Hopefully, no more will be lost. Profit has taken a bad turn.

Having a crew that *"is not stellar"* does not help. Two have turned out to be thieves, *"what a pair to fall to my lot,"* and his nephew, William Thompson, as first mate, is more a hindrance than a help. He terms him *"a dunce"* and vows to never have him on another voyage whether his sister Dorothy likes it or not.

A trip to shore finds him unable to replenish his stores of water and corn because many vessels are seeking refuge and provisions are scarce. After dining at the British Consulate he hurries back to the ship. He must head out to sea. The holiday season and violent weather have caused too many ships and small vessels to congregate in the harbour and off shore. Three vessels are lost, one with all on board. Only the Captain's skills see them safely on their way.

1820

The winter of 1820 brings change in Britain. Word that King George III has died prompts William to say that *"the country would have been better if he had died at twenty not eighty."* People are in a very bad way, poverty and sickness abound. Perhaps a new monarch can turn things around.

Mary hopes that Ned's marriage to Elizabeth Clarkson will be a good match. At home two things are causing her concern. Eliza's hormones are causing some natural problems and Mary doesn't always believe that the young lady is telling the truth about her activities with boys. More importantly, the fact that William has agreed to bring Robert Hornell back from Antigua to be their charge while he attends boarding school is not something she has envisioned. A five year old boy, who is bound to be homesick, creates a challenge she does not need.

By the end of February William is again having problems with his crew. *"My love, I have had an uneasy week. I have put my last foremast man in jail and yesterday, Gibson, the boatswain. He has acted like a thorough rascal. He is 17 shillings, 6 pence in the ship's debt. So much for my kindness to him. It's a long story. I assure you, Mary, I am not the least in fault. He brought it on himself. I have now got six men from St John's and hope will go on better. Tom Bowling got leave to see a relation in St. John's about three weeks ago and has never come back. I understand they keep a grog shop and the boy will be ruined by attending. I am advised to get him back, which I will do, out of compassion. He lived with the steward and was treated kindly, never got a blow, but once, and that for repeatedly neglecting things he was told to do. Gratitude is rarely found these days."* Tom did come back only to have to appear before a Magistrate. The little ungrateful imp had stolen clothes on false pretenses.

He vows to *"inculcate better principles into our dear boy"* and expresses his love in a poem.

> *"What words can speak the bright emotion*
> *That sparkled in his Father's eyes*
> *When to his fond paternal bosom*
> *He proudly pressed his darling boy."*

He begs Mary to wean the baby so that she may go with him on the next voyage either to Antigua or to St. Petersburg, preferably to the south. He knows that she would enjoy another warm holiday and a visit with her island friends. If, as planned, his mother comes to London to live with them he fears that she will not look after the children and let Mary get away.

Finally, March 9, 1820, the Antaeus is on its way home with the hope of a four week trip. A night of the *"longest and heaviest rain I ever knew has made a bad beginning, they say, oft times makes a good ending."* His nephew, he vows, will never sail with him again. *"A robber is an honest man where he comes. Ship's stores, provisions, and everything is alike sacrificed by him."* He intends to tell his sister Dorothy that her son is lazy, undependable and a common thief.

As always William is impatient to get home. *"Oh my dear Mary, my heyday of blood is over. I cannot now amuse myself by building castles in the air. My thoughts are nothing now but plain matters of fact. I am tired, indeed of this wandering sort of life."*

The winds do not cooperate and May 16th finds the Antaeus *"100 miles behind my reckoning. She so badly steered that it would deceive anyone to account for her real rate of sailing. We have had a strong gale at NNW for five days, running in the rough of the sea but no other damage done. I would not heave to."*

Mary needs a break and William again begs her to be on the next voyage with him.

"My love, there is not a day to lose. I hope your preparations for the voyage are made. It will be a short one as we must leave Antigua by August 1ˢᵗ, not an hour must be wasted. I have carried sail all the passage, like when I was a young fellow. Tell Mother if Ned is married, I don't give up my idea that Mother and self are still the handsomest of the family."

The couple look forward to their holiday but November finds William, without Mary, on his way to Antigua. She is pregnant again! This time the Antaeus is Noah's Ark carrying rabbits, cats, a fox terrier, horses and asses. With any luck they will all live.

On all things even the Captain cannot win and finds that his crafty nephew had been busy *"unrigging the ship;"* every rope had to be spliced. The disappointed Captain, to say the least, is not pleased.

1821

Sometime during this period Mary opens a shop, The Ship's Chandler & Co., No. 120, Cock Hill, Radcliffe, London. It is registered to William's name and provides trade with the locals, the Islands and seafaring people. Her inventory is varied, oils, colours, boatswain's stores, carpenter's stores, steward's and cook's supplies and gunner's needs as well as dry goods such as the cheap clothing known as slops, sea beds and bedding. It is really "a one place stop to shop."

W. BYERS,
SHIP CHANDLER, &c.
No. 120, COCK HILL, RATCLIFF.

SELLS THE FOLLOWING GOODS,

(Original document - Byers family collection)

Sending ladies' things to the islands suffers a setback when, in early summer, her friend, Mrs. Rogers, sends back unsold merchandise and remits only a fraction of its worth, thinking it better to sell for less instead of returning the goods. Three yards of returned tassnett is to be dyed a darker blue and made into a fashionable evening dress because its blue is *"too pale for the night."* Friends expect a lot but Mary, being Mary, will do her best to have it ready to send back when William leaves again in October.

July 4, 1821, Mary gives birth to a healthy daughter, Anne. A letter dated November 8, 1821, confirms the date when Mary says, "*our dear Anne has cut a tooth, found it only yesterday being four months and three days old.*" Family and friends, again, wonder how this young woman finds any time for herself.

October 8, 1821. William safely runs the Needles, the three sharp pointed rocks off the coast of the Isle of Wight. Having forgotten to leave behind a copy of his accounts he has angered and frustrated his wife. If only he would try harder she would not be so vexed. Never holding a grudge, she scolds him and sends him a cap and lovingly wishes him well. Ned, who has not been well and has not yet made a living with his doctoring, is again part of the crew. The Antaeus, in wild, cold seas, peppered by hailstones is carrying passengers who are not weathering the strong north gale well. The Captain believes had he not docked at Falmouth they would have been dead. He quips, "*so much for the south of England being the place for invalids in winter.*"

Christmas finds Mary feeling as if she is writing to a shadow. Sad accounts of dreadful gales causing severe damage to shipping have reached her. She doesn't know if he is safe, healthy or on his way home. William's nightly dreaming of his father, more nightmare than dream, makes her wonder how the trusty Antaeus will get him home.

The bad weather is not just at sea. Violent rains have inundated half the town. *"Our kitchens have been under water eleven days. We just got the Christmas dinner dressed, the women wearing patens whilst attending to it, when we were compelled to turn the back parlour into a kitchen, where*

Mistress Charlotte has held court ever since. The hurricanes in the West Indies cannot exceed the violence of gales experienced in England in the last two months. We read in the papers of fifty full grown oak trees, forming an avenue to a gentleman's house, uprooted last Friday by the violence of the storm , and a thousand other accounts, equally terrific but too long for detailing here."

News that the Thompson family has possibly lost a vessel will be of interest to William. Even though he seldom wishes Robert well his sister needs no further stress in her life.

1822

The new year, 1822, sweeps in with more bad weather from the west. They both say, *"Do not think when it is bad with you, 'tis possible the same wind cannot affect us"*. Worry is never far away.

February 6th, Mary finally knows that in spite of accounts of losses at sea William has safely reached Antigua. Their parting had not been amicable, *"no sympathy existed between us this time of our parting. But love begets love."*

She is not one to hold a grudge and goes on to tell him about the children. *"William is a treasure, stout Ann, with four teeth is the picture of health, Eliza is dancing again and Robert Hornell is well."* She is not pregnant and tells her husband, *"thanks for not permitting me to arrive at that point of weakness."* She looks forward to a healthy, happy winter.

Thrilled to be part of the birth of Ned's daughter she tells William of the hair-raising time. *"The little stranger was not expected until quite the latter end of the month, and coming on first occasioned a little additional bustle, as the watchman called past one o'clock and before we knew what was the matter and before two all was over. Edward is to know that his sister has more than an aunt's share in this babe, wishes God to bless it and hopes it will prove comfort to him in his old age."*

William brings home treasures - shells, skins, and shawls. This time she is thrilled to learn that for £13 he has bought a five piece dining room set, *"the table capable of dining above a dozen. Should they not suit, they will always fetch the money. I felt a pleasure in doing it."*

Valentine's Day always brings out the romance in William and feeling lonely he writes

> *"The treasures of the deep are not so precious*
> *as are the concealed comforts of a man*
> *locked up in woman's love, I scent the air,*
> *of blessing, when I come but near the house.*
> *What a delicious breath marriage sends forth,*
> *the violet's bed's not sweeter."*

He continues, *"I have been unable to stoop forward to write for more than a week with a kick from a horse under my ribs, but am now writing without any pain. It pinched me for a few days."* The crops are so slow that he will not be able to sail before April. He can't get a bill of sale so he can't send her any money. He still has a mare to sell and money to collect from the sale of the asses. Letters like this are sometimes hard to take. Hopefully he will not give in to the idea that smoking his cigars from St. Thomas will help fill in his lonely evenings. He admits that his *"temper doesn't suit the shuffling of knaves."*

On the bright side, for the trip home, he has passengers at thirty pounds sterling each. The downside is that he has lost thirty pounds and Ned one hundred dollars when they raced *"the wherry against Captain Head's boat."* Now he must try to find more passengers which unfortunately will take several weeks. Time is not his friend!

The Antaeus returns home safely and with it comes an order from Jane Ottley, a welcome boost for Mary's business. It is an intriguing request, a wonderful assortment of treasured goods that could not be found on the island: 3 yards of plain bobbin cut yard wide, not to exceed 7/ per yard; 15 yards of narrow edging for ruffs, about one shilling per yard; 2 figured pink Barcelona handkerchiefs [whole ones]; 2 bottles of Delcroix Lavender; 4

pairs of long white gloves; 6 pair of short coloured kid gloves; 6 papers of short pins; 6 papers a size larger.

Jane closes her letter with *"I have many thanks to return for your present of preserves which Captain Byers delivered to me. He has been detained much longer than he expected in consequence of our unfortunate bad crops. Indeed, many ships have been obliged to leave the island without getting a single hogshead of sugar but we hope next year will be better."*

January 1823

Although fierce winter weather at the Downs had caused *"a near termination of his voyage and perhaps his life."* William is safe and Mary's life, though busy, seems to be easier. She amuses her husband with female chit-chat. She has help in the shop and at home. William is at school at Mrs. Brock's and doing well. She tells her husband that her mind is easier and that she seems to rely on him with more perfect confidence now than she had been able to in the last five years. All this contributes to make both her spirits and her bodily health much better.

February 5th Mary's home news is again positive as she tells William that they have all recovered from colds and are as well as *"you could wish us. William begs me to tell you he is a gentleman, only wants a pony you promised him to ride about on next summer, and the ship to sail on the canal, then he shall be very happy, for you will manage it for him. Eliza is well and Anne is round and happy, finally saying 'Mama.' I should feel uneasy did she not understand everything said to her."*

The deaths of old friends are related along with the names of those who inherit the estates; she is doing well collecting money to enable the Clark boy to enrol in Bancroft's School. Shepherd left London on Christmas Day and William's family in the north are all well, his mother better than all the rest. February's weather is severe on the north coast with vessels lost and William's brother-in-law, Charles Thompson, fears the loss of his son, William, and his ship, the Ajax. Thompson has just returned from Pictou,

Nova Scotia carrying white pine timber for the masts of ships and wood for decking. Hopefully William will be interested in the fact that *"many boats are being chartered for Quebec and the Baltic."* Such trips would be much shorter than the ones to the West Indies. Anything to get away from the long voyages to the islands should be considered.

Black clouds are looming. *"There is much talk of war at present. I heard the other day of a person who had nearly engaged to charter his vessel but withdrew, intending to reserve her for transport service. So sanguine are some people, but you will hear more about it from the public papers than I am able to inform you."*

Mary is pregnant again, busy with her shop, and worried about William keeping his affairs on an even path. Her three active children leave few moments to herself. She carries her baby well and in July presents William with another son, Richard Dudderidge Byers. She was busy before, she will be busier now!

William's time in Antigua, as usual, is beset with trials and tribulations that even follow him home. Late season storms cause much damage to the sugars leaving profit slim and tensions high. Dealings with Mr. Swanson, his partner, cause a rift leaving William no longer connected to the Antaeus and in the market for another new brig.

1824

The BENJAMIN

In February's very cold stormy weather on his new brig Benjamin, our Mariner reports *"winds round the compass"* and is heading to Yarmouth to mail *"a much promised letter."* He doesn't wonder that North Country seamen are rough; they have rough elements with which to contend. If the winds allow him to land he knows that the port will be crowded. Ships are *"tied so close that one can walk from ship to ship along the coastline."*

Between South Shields and the Downs, after three sleepless nights that found the Captain with "*no lights to be seen*" he lands at Yarmouth.

> *"The sea made a fair breach over us. In this part of the deeps the sea gives a small ship no chance, it being nothing but broken water. I know the worst part of the passage is past and have every confidence in the vessel altho' she made a great deal of water when she began to pitch. In the ocean she will live like a duck. I have bought a new pair of sea boots and am in a hurry to get on board."*

In hopes of a letter from home before setting out to sea, he will check the post office at the Downs. Manipulating the Downs is always a challenge. The chalky Cliffs of Dover can be a wonder to see but storms from every direction can drive ships onto the shore and the drifting sands.

In February their letters cross paths at sea, William's of the 4th and 6th match Mary's of the 5th.

James Dudderidge has dined with members of the Club in which the Benjamin is insured and some regulations have changed. The day of sailing from the West Indies is prolonged till the 24th or 25th of August so that no vessel should be allowed to make more than three voyages in the coal trade. The former of those provisions makes it no longer doubtful that there is plenty of time for William to make a second voyage this year.

> *"God grant it may prove so, when we shall have some prospect of making a little provision for old age, and our children likewise will not be left destitute. I do urge you, my dear Byers, to endeavour all in your power not to disappoint my expectations, convinced as I am you will do it for principal alone."*

Eliza is seventeen and like all adolescents, though respectful, is a bit of a handful. If she has time to spend idle hours with a boyfriend Mary believes that it is time for her to learn a trade. A Memorandum of Agreement between Mary May and Mary Byers is drawn up in the presence of Elizabeth Huxtable and Sarah May. Eliza's free time is no more.

*"Memorandum of Agreement made this day between Mary Byers of
Crown Row, on the one part, and Miss Mary May, of the same
place, on the other. Mary Byers agrees to place her daughter,
Elizabeth Stephenson Byers, with Miss May for the term of one
year from the date hereof to learn the business of Millinery, Dress,
and Pelisse making in all its branches, her hours of employment to
be from nine in the morning 'till eight in the evening coming home
to all her meals, except Tea, likewise to sleep at home, and that she
shall not on any pretext be suffered to run errands or carry out
parcels, and in consideration of which, Mary Byers agrees to pay
Miss May the sum of five pounds, and it is mutually understood
that in the event of Miss May failing to fulfill her part of the
covenant that she shall return one half of the paid sum."* May
24th, 1824

William hopes that this will soften his daughter's temperament. One of her
friends is to be well married and he feels that a less fiery demeanour would
help her gain a suitable match.

By June 11, 1824, in Jamaica this voyage, nothing is going well for
William.

*"Having no negroes employed the people are slow to provide and
slow to load a cargo of 100 puncheons of rum, 20 hogsheads of
rum and 10 tierces of sugar."*

Loneliness sets in and he thinks until he gets into the coal trade nothing
will go right for him.

*"The other afternoon I thought to myself, I am not sleepy, I am not
hungry, yet I want something. At last I found it was to lay my head
in my Mary's knee. I want to make money but it is at the expense of
my happiness."*

He is anxious to be loaded by the end of June so that he can get to Belfast
and back by Christmas with cargo for Mary's Christmas sales. He begs Mary
to meet him at Liverpool and go with him to Belfast.

A visit to Kingston, Jamaica, in very heavy rains, finds him stranded for the night at Mr. Bayly's £200,000 estate. He feels it a privilege as he is the only captain who ever dines and *"takes a bed"* in Gibraltar Castle. *"My offhand manner pleases some people. Bayly's house is really grand. His wife is a good sort of woman and well read. She helps conversation by many sensible remarks. Was he in better health, I should be much with him."*

It's time for some rest and recuperation. He visits the Blue Mountains that run from one end of the island to the other.

> *"You would enjoy the romantic valleys, the rich appearance of this valuable island which fanaticism would wrest from old England. Here the people have taken a stand against the ministry and now make laws and govern themselves. They are Britons, the bright jewel of the British Crown. It is hoped that the people of England will realize the value of Jamaica and the West Indies in preference to the East Indies, which is only a drain on the mother country, both for money and seamen. People of Annotto Bay are not known for their hospitality."*

He hadn't been told that the Benjamin leaked so badly and wonders that they had not gone down with it on the passage. He refers to his usual luck, *"not born to be drowned."* He hopes that with the caulking of forty trinnels it will be tight for the voyage home.

He wants Mary packed and ready to join him for the trip to Belfast when he docks in Liverpool. *"You know my anxious temper when in the same country with you."*

Pirates terrorizing and plundering ships in Annotto Bay strand the impatient Captain for 11 days creating more problems. His mate, *"a sluggard, a drunkard, a fool and a mad man"* has abandoned ship, leaving the vessel shorthanded to fight hurricane strength winds when they finally leave the island on August 15th.

Finally, home safe and sound their lives follow a yearly pattern of family time and work. 1824 slips away like all years do and the new one is greeted with optimism.

Trouble for the Benjamin

Newhaven, February 11, 1825

On the Benjamin, near Newhaven, the folly of sleepy crewmen on watch causes a near disaster. Mary reads the story.

"I wrote you a short letter from Lowes yesterday, where I was about the protest. The expenses will amount to near the cost of the damage. I can give you a more cool detail, but there was not the least danger to life. Therefore I cannot be grateful to God for preserving me to my family a little longer, but I am truly grateful for being spared the mortification of losing a vessel in such a silly, boyish way. I was on deck at least three times in the night, and between 5 and 6 came up again a fine clear morning, the moon shining bright, standing in for the land which near to Beach Head, you know how high and white it is, it could barely be seen. I told the fellow I gave passage to in St. Thomas, whom I had appointed to keep my watch, in presence of the carpenter, to let me know in good time to put the ship about as she drew near to the land. I fell asleep, and about one half past seven, he came and told me, she was to Brighton Pier. I asked if the lead had been hove. He said this - there were three fathoms and no wind. Up I jumped, hove over the lead, the two fathom mark above water, immediately down anchor, and it proved dead low water. As the flood made, it began to blow from the SW. I could not cast to take sail until high water, without a change of wind and sea increased, and I slacked away cable just keeping her from striking the ground. Well, when she came head to the sea at high water, she pitched so heavy as to occasion the palls of the windlass to give way as in the Queen's Channel, and thought all would have torn away together.

[I] was inclined to boast, all that seamanship could do was done, to keep her fast one half an hour longer when the tide would enable us to ship and make sail. The cable was slashed in every possible way to hold her, and thank God, I succeeded.

I got a boat off, who I had sent away before, and with as much coolness as Nelson at Copenhagen, when he rejected wafer and called for sealing wax, insisted on a written agreement and laughed at the fellows, who seeing who they had to deal with, candidly said they would take thirty pounds, altho' they had intended to ask three hundred pounds.

I had a spring in the cable and all prepared. My intention was to run to the Downs, but they told me of Newhaven, and recollected reading in my Naval Chronicle, how the harbour was improved so, for 30 pounds, they assisted to get the ship into a safe port, and when the weather moderated to fetch the anchor and 45 fathoms of cable.

The exertion when it was over, cost me dear. It shook me much, but today I am, I may say, as usual. A few bales of goods are partially damaged owing to the strain on the Bitt Heads, but cannot affect the ship. I have taken every care by survey.

It has been calm today, but a breeze has sprung up from the SW. Write by return. One has no choice, one must carry on."

Nothing Goes Well

In the spring of 1825, Antigua is plagued with setbacks. Everything on the island has ground to a halt - rainy weather, Easter, a Jewish holiday, no slaves working, no help to be had, and most frustrating of all, special treatment given to a large vessel, the *Camden*. Having arrived earlier than others, no one else can begin loading until the large ship is finished. The three week wait is long and tedious. William says that if he had made three coal voyages and then come to Antigua he would have been finished earlier. Having made a side trip to Kingston, Jamaica has put him behind the Camden, the Topaze, the George Hibbert, the Killingbeck and the Antaeus.

Prospects in Antigua are much altered. Where William is used to getting 100 hogsheads, now only 10 or 20 have emerged after a frustrating wait. Having the mate put sugar where the molasses should go and vice versa really hasn't helped. Give him the coal trade, or any trade, rather than this inactive life.

He is worried about Mary. She is again pregnant and he says, *"I shall get a shawl for you and praying God to protect my dear Mary thro' her approaching peril, I suppose early in July."*

In June, after shedding a gallon of sweat for every hogshead of sugar he gets, he rides to Stony Hill and then across the upcountry to Cassada Gardens. Crossing a swamp his horse becomes stuck and in trying to extricate itself throws him over its head, landing on his left leg.

> *"I was afraid of his getting his forefeet on me as a support, and so pass over me, but, God be thanked, I was able to spring away like a monkey."*

Even with a great deal of discomfort William keeps going until he reaches the highest point on the island where he camps for the night. In the morning, well rested he bathes in a pond and then, to his disappointment, a dense haze obliterates the view of the twelve islands that he had come to see.

Still frustrated by delays, on July 23rd he finds himself still on the island feeling sure that Mary has delivered her baby. *"I trust in God that this shall find you safe recovered from your confinement and me the father of another healthy babe."* A second wee Mary did arrive safely on the 24th, his premonition was correct.

For six weeks rain and more rain bring things almost to a standstill. The rain does not let up causing the fields to be under water; the Freeman's estate being entirely under water. Horses get stuck in the mud forcing the servants to carry sugar cane to the mill on their heads. Desperate, he sets out by horse on a thirty mile ride to visit inland plantations in hope of the promise of sugars. The only answer he gets is *"we would be glad to ship, had we sugars."* He has loaded 68 hogsheads and 25 tierces but doubts he will not exceed £800. Ships have come that will not be loaded until November. He has been given a promise that if he is in Antigua next January he will be loaded and able to sail immediately.

Time is running out. He must be ready to sail by August 15th. Hurricanes season is approaching and his insurance will be invalidated if he tarries longer on the island. He must have a full ship, but it isn't promising. There is too much competition and too little sugar.

Finally, September 8th, 1825, the Benjamin, is at sea, 1000 miles from the *"Land's End of Old England."* Mary reads again of *"horrors of the sea."*

> *"I left Antigua on the 15th of August and the next day I sprang a leak in the stern port, twelve inches of water on the rod. I resolved on the bold measure of finding shelter among the keys of Anguilla, smooth water being all I wanted. Well, I succeeded in passing between the reefs, the sea breaking on them mountains high, and brought my vessel to anchor where never European vessel was before, when to my surprise [I] found a Custom House Officer, also holding the position of Notary Public etc., etc. [I] soon got the leak stopped, but had to note a pretest of six dollars. I beat out among the reefs, against the advice of the people, who said I was most fortunate in getting safe in thro' them before the wind, but the wind was ahead in a safer channel. To a North Country Seaman, it seemed nothing. Although it completely answered my purpose and as I never can have a knack of making money by strangers, either for myself or others, I must take some little credit to myself and still lay my head down in my own world and sleep an honest man, without the help of either trick or priest craft or any extraordinary powers, only common sense, and what you deny me, application to my duty. Had started out in a strong westerly, what some would call a hurricane, but it did not blow as hard as when coming from Belfast."*

The Captain's luck did not hold. Forces beyond the trusty Benjamin's control swamped the labouring brig and brought it to its heels. Despite a heroic effort on the part of captain and crew the snapping of masts and the listing of the vessel were telling the tale that might never be told. An angry Poseidon was winning. As the water crested and swamped the deck, the howling wind outcried the pleas of the bell, the call of the horn and the terror-filled cries of the crew. Shipwreck in mid-Atlantic seemed inevitable.

Was this how it would end? William, with thoughts of his dear Mary and his bairns, prayed as he had never prayed before.

Time was an eternity..... and yet there seemed to be so little of it available.

THE BENJAMIN IS GOING DOWN!

The day is September 26,1825 and the Captain's luck does not hold. Forces beyond the trusty Benjamin's control swamp the laboring brig and bring it to its heels. Despite a heroic effort on the part of the captain and crew the snapping of masts and the listing of the vessel tell a tale that might never be told.

An angry Poseidon is winning. As the water crests and swamps the deck the howling wind outcries the pleas of the bell, the call of the horn and the terror filled cries of the crew. Shipwreck in the mid Atlantic seems inevitable.

Time is an eternity and yet there seems to be so little of it available. Was this how it will end? William, with thoughts of his "dear Mary and his bairns", prays as he had never prayed before.

Providentially, when all seems lost, the murky shape of the South Shield's vessel, "the John Twizzel" quickly bares down on them and in a flash of time, as another mast crashes around their heads and the sea overpowers the deck, the captain, crew and dog are plucked from the long arm of death.

Not until October the second does William have time to sit down and in his own words tells Mary of his harrowing experience. Meanwhile the coastal gossip mill carries the tale south, retells it again and again causing much grief to waiting family. In tears Mary pleads *"there has to be a better way"*.

1826, The Brig Ann

No More Antigua

It was Captain William's last voyage to Antigua and the Islands. With Mary's insistence his focus shifts to the coal trade. But without a ship, you can dream and plan all you want but not a single coal will you transport.

January 1826 finds him without enough money to buy a ship and no available vessel for him to command. William writes *"Mr. Byers is in London and George Ramsey cannot command enough money to get a vessel without more money on my part. The command of a vessel in any trade doesn't offer and except the help I can be to the shop might as well have remained in London. I have taken my passage from here in the Commerce belonging to Stanhope, and trust to get away in the morning tide."* He doesn't take kindly to idleness and tells Mary that he is *"harassed out of my life about nothing."*

Finally, April 18th, much to Mary's relief a new Brig, the Ann, gives William back his pride and garners a new sense of freedom and adventure within him. Although *"it is too slow for the Trade Winds"* he has faith that his profits will increase. It's a different ship, in need of repair and alteration of sails. While he waits to load coal near Newcastle he moves the mainmast aft and lengthens the sails. Like waiting for sugars he must wait for *"a turn of coals."* It's all bustle or idleness and next time he will know how to use the unusual stowing space to its best advantage. At least in the north he is not always alone. He knows the area and he knows many people; family, friends and co-workers. Depression plagues him much less frequently.

Archangel, Russia

Most coal voyages go south to service the London area but Captain William wishes to sample the Baltic trade, hopefully getting all the way to Archangel (present day St. Petersburg) in Russia. He gets that chance and July 25, 1826, safely arrives in Archangel, Russia.

The trip is long and arduous to reach Arkhangelsk, in the very north of European Russia. From Shields the charts take him north through the North Sea, along the coast of Norway, through the Barents Sea, over the top of Norway and Finland and then south through the Norwegian Sea to the White Sea. Archangel is only accessible during the summer months, where the average temperature is fifty nine degrees and daylight only briefly fades into twilight. The English have traded with the people in this area since the sixteenth century. The heavily forested area provides timber to be taken south to the British Isles to sustain the British shipbuilding trade. These Baltic voyages are much shorter in time than those to the East and West Indies and soon he is back in England.

Time passes. September 23, 1826, William, on the Isle of Glosh, Cheapstow, near Bristol is, as always, happy to hear that his crew at home are well and that money is not a problem.

Mary's shop is improving *"tho' not as yet supporting us entirely"* being helped by a new customer, a new friend William has made in the port of Archangel, *"who has promised his custom to the shop."* She now has, due to Charles Thompson taking a large shipment of her stock, an exciting new market in St. Petersburg.

At home, Mary is concerned about Ned, the ne'er-do-well surgeon/chemist who is ill. Ned and his family have fallen on hard times. They are mourning the death of their baby boy, George, *"who expired before the nurse could get down stairs with him."* With no place to live, Mary has opened the doors of her already crowded home to Ned, Betsey and their children. She knows that William will not be happy about this and begs him not to quarrel. *"I would rather they had not been here when you returned, but had not the heart to say no."*

Alarmingly, William's last letter had told of very wet, disagreeable weather and that a mishap of some kind had caused injury to his right eye. In a gale, the beam of the main mast has swung around and whacked him in the head badly damaging his eye. Another calamity; she hopes that he does not feel any inconvenience from the blow in his eye. *"You do not mention it in your last, therefore conclude it is not worse, at all events."*

William is concerned that the children will be very much afraid of him. *"I fear I will look very much changed."*

William has been very concerned about Eliza's habit of being less than truthful about her suitor and is most interested to hear the details. *"The boy's father's connections are respected, he is a coal merchant and lighterman."* The young swain is sixteen and perhaps an apprentice to his father. They probably met at the stairs opposite the coal barges. Hopefully now that William is in the loop Mary believes that she will have fewer problems with her step-daughter. *"Eliza is too much in a hurry and lessens herself by the encouragement she gives."* Mary believes that Eliza's age, personal attractions, and respectability command something better than this.

Robert Hornell, their ward from Antigua, sent to England to complete his studies, is troublesome and unruly at times. He has hurt his leg and being *"an invalid has not had his clothes on for a fortnight."* The fact that he is now putting his foot on the ground gives hope that the Doctor was wrong in anticipating that the boy would not regain the use of the leg. Having been advised by Mr. Eddington, *"who is very high in the list of Hospital Surgeons,"* Mary is confident she has done the very best she can for the boy in her care.

Little Mary is improving quickly and Bill, having spent a fortnight with Uncle William Clarkson is *"quite on his legs again."* Young Dick says that his Father has made him a Captain and will buy him a ship by and by.

Kind words from the Indies assure the Captain that a man's reputation always follows in his wake but kind words from Antigua do not entice him to head south again.

1827

The next year is seemingly uneventful, just hard slugging and more of the same.

The voyages to the south were longer and cursed with the frustrations of tedium but the northern ones have proven to be much more dangerous with the challenges of severe weather. A letter from William, sent from Monkwearmouth, near Sunderland, has shocked his family.

Disaster has befallen the Brig Ann. The loss of ship and cargo are an *"unavoidable misfortune."* Monkwearmouth is a ship building port so hopefully Mary will hear that something can be salvaged. She quickly writes to William.

> *"That your letter has shocked and affected me, it is in vain to deny, but when I look round on our healthy children and think that they are not fatherless, my sorrow is turned into thankfulness, and I bless God for his infinite mercies. True, it is a great loss, but I trust something will yet turn out for our advantage. Do not, therefore, repine at unavoidable misfortune. We have still our youth and health on our side, and if we are doomed to work for daily bread, do not, I again repeat, grieve at it. We will bring our children up to industry that they may never know the disappointments we have experienced. Endeavor to be reconciled to circumstances. Our little ones are all well. William, when I told him what had happened, inquired first for you, then if all the sailors were saved, and lastly for the poor dog. On my telling him all was saved, he burst into tears. I should not write hoping you will have left with Captain Reay, but if not, think it will be a comfort to you to hear from home."*

Mary learns the details of the catastrophe when his letter of the 20th arrives.

> *"The hull of the poor Ann was sold yesterday for £61. All the stores were saved and sent to Shields where they sold for a fifth of the proceeds, say £50 to £100 in addition to the £800 insured - but it's poor comfort for the loss of such a firm good vessel. I entirely*

despair of ever being able to replace her at all. I don't think she would have sustained any considerable injury even from the rocks had not the other large ships pressed her on them. One went to pieces and the other not much better.

The Ann may be got off - but her repairs would exceed the sum insured - and that would not have suited me - we have made the best of the job. The other two saved little.

I exerted myself when I did not know I would benefit anything from my efforts. I thank God no fault can be found with me. When I paid the sailors' wages I had only about £2 left. Had I given way to the carpenter and part of the crew and left the ship in the boats we would all have perished. Only the mate and one man were sterling.

I cannot yet form any idea when I can leave this place, indeed, my Darling, I would like a little time elapse before we meet. Until things are sold I can come to no settlement with the Clubs and whether when I leave without the proceeds of sale - whether it would be remitted punctually - they seem fair.

My mind is much relieved from writing this. I have kept my dog. Reay wanted to bring him home to you but I could not part with him."

Mary knows her husband; he has been badly shaken and probably not telling the whole story. Time will tell. Pride takes a downturn with any wreck or accident. A new brig means money is needed up front, always a problem, but once more accomplished.

1829 On the Brig Betsey

There are no letters from November 1827 to March 18, 1829 when we hear of another close call. On his new Brig Betsey they have found refuge in Sunderland's hectic harbour where a very anxious William tells the story.

"I arrived here yesterday afternoon and got in with about £2 damage, thank God. At one moment, the ship would have been

knocked to pieces. It's beyond the memory of man, such a throng of ships and so much damage done.

I steered her in myself, and she lay as fair as a ship could do, when a steamboat took the brig below us in tow, and run into our stern, upsetting all our steering apparatus, lower masts, bowsprits, and sterns into the water's edge. Indeed, some suffered at both ends, and a schooner hardly floated up the harbour, but an end to the dismals. Through a throng of ships we manoeuvered when at one moment the ship would have been knocked to pieces. Mr. Byers fixed me with Hettons for ten shillings, nine pence freight. It was an anxious time. To anchor was to risk everything as many did. To run for Shields, call it what you will, forbid me. I last told him to make up his mind, either to anchor or take the harbour, but no hesitation, the way seemed clear, and we pushed in, and would not get a scratch but for the wrong conduct of a steamer, and nothing. My not having spare money prevents me punishing him for it."

He is happy with his new brig. *"Confirmed my good opinion of her. Sails very fair, indeed many will reckon her very fast."*

March 25, 1829, finds the Betsey loaded with coal and anchored at Lowestaffe, the most easterly point of England, being beaten by a NW wind. Snow and terrific gales have kept him from sailing and *"he is all out of patience."*

"We suppose no ships have got down, and they must have had a cold, beating time of it. We have worn nothing but provisions and patience. The decks are covered with snow, but it is a fine morning, and shall take the opportunity of seeing the new harbour they are making."

One must admire the resilience of both William and Mary. So many times William's letters tell of hardship due to severe conditions beyond his control but a bit of sunshine gets him going again and Mary, hearing all of this, has no choice but to set worry aside, write encouraging letters and keep everything on an even keel.

Long lay overs for any reason are costly. Insurance must be added, provisions of beef, bread and other necessities must be refurbished, depleting the profits before they even start for home.

His mind goes back to the terror of Sunderland Harbour.

> *"Indeed, my dear Mary, it required good courage, as well as perseverance to take Sunderland Harbour at such a time, and, between ourselves, another time will run to Shields. About 40 Sunderland ships did so. At one moment I thought she would have been knocked to pieces and thought my fate hard enough, but, thank God escaped with small loss. The main boom I don't replace, have altered the sail to do without tithe, new tiller only cost 9 shillings, the sky light about £5, but, as it was intended to be done, it has only hurried the thing, and the timber in the cellar will repair the little that is wanted in the strength. Club has ordered a new topsail, which I got off Mrs. Oliver and a main sail, which I got here."*

Economic times, all over England, are worsening. He knows that when he gets home there will be rent to pay, sugar wanted and Mary's needs to be considered. He is very uneasy about it all and feels it is *"useless to think about it."*

The Stephenson's, his first wife's family, are a continuing concern even though the never ending settlement of Ann's will now shows some promise. A copy is finally promised for the next voyage and the affair is to be closed as soon as possible. He doubts that by now there is anything left for his daughter; the family will have eaten it all away. *"George Stephenson takes a passage with me, determined to get anything in any way. If he doesn't immediately get a master's berth, we will not ask him to leave the ship to come to the house - enough of that last year."*

Waiting is again an aggravation so Sunday evening William writes again to *"My dear Mary."*

> *"I got loaded on Friday. She took twelve keels and two chaldrons, but loaded so much by the stern as could not fill her. Another*

voyage now I know her trim will take 13 keels, a little under thirteen feet of water, and will make an excellent collier. I am now, my love, well tired with this harbour. I came into it in a throng and have to lay loaded, the sea high and the tides bad. She has a good berth and (so I) don't complain. It's a long voyage, but I thank God sincerely, all is yet well. The Bridget will get a voyage, but I have acted on the principle we agreed on, and however galling to be outdone by Boobys I still consider them as they are Boobys. Perhaps Mr. Byers' funds, and many others, are as little able to encounter misfortunes as my own, and wear and tear, have had none. I have dined with Mr. Byers and got on board before dark, but having ate my supper, (I) am not inclined to write longer, but will have time enough before there is any chance of getting to sea. Good night, my wife."

Bad weather continues until Wednesday, a few do get away and another note is in the making.

"Seven small vessels got away this afternoon, one of which stuck on the Bar and is at anchor in the Roads, with men sent to pump her until she can get in again. Such a job would not suit my funds. The wind is now NW with snow and frost, which at night draws the wind off the land, but it is still northeasterly at sea. Should the sea fall in the course of the night may, as the tides are now good, get away tomorrow day tide. She is now 13 feet, 5 inches water. Mr. Byers got them to increase my freight to 11 shillings when I signed the charter, and clear of brokerage. I have little more to say. Wm. Byers has just left me, and it is bed time." (Mr. Byers is a cousin.)

Thursday *"The sea is higher. None can get away."* The weather is still unsettled but ships do sail in the next few days. Idleness is never productive and chances, at times, must be taken.

The Loss of the Betsey

News of seafaring people travels up and down the coast by whichever ship arrives first at port. Mary is home, pregnant, busy with her children and her shop, when she hears that *"the Brig Betsey is lost."* Fear immobilizes the entire household. Stories are embellished with the telling. What can one believe?

A letter, dated April 15, 1829, from Pakefield, near Lowestoft finally arrives but it is not from William.

> *"Madam,*
>
> *Captain William Byers requests me to write to you a few lines, to say he is quite well, but has not been enabled to write to you time enough for the post. You will no doubt have heard of the loss of the Betsey yesterday. All the crew are saved, and I believe most of the clothes etc. As Captain Byers will write you in a day or two and give you the particulars, I must to save the Post, only say, I remain,*
>
> *Your obedient servant,*
>
> *G. S. Gawrey*
>
> *You will please direct any letters to be left at my office Lowestoft."*

Why doesn't he write? What is wrong?

William's letter of April 14th, 1829 from Pakefield, near Lowestaffe, tells us just how upset Mary must have been.

> *"My dear Mary,*
>
> *Yours of yesterday has just come to hand. I wrote to you yesterday, but as you request me to write by return, and for the fear any miscarriage occurs to the other, I send this as another day's uneasiness must not be thought of. Indeed, my love, I cannot comprehend how you could at all imagine we were all gone. The report at Lloyd's could not possibly lead to any such conclusion. I sent George Stephenson on shore with all our clothes on Sunday*

forenoon, but had not the presence of mind to tell him to write to you, nor did he ever think of it himself.

I have little to say, in addition to yesterday, only the protest is completed, and it blows a strong gale at south, and the ship nearly under water, with a heavy sea breaking over her. She stands and has stood to wonder. Mr. Gawrey says any new Sunderland built ship would not have stood it two hours, but her goodness is now of little avail to me. You are to tell John Stephenson, his brother has made his mind up to return to Shields from this. The moment any idea can be formed when I can leave this I will let you know. We expect letters from the Clubs [insurance] on Friday. And about the cargo, I am not obliged to see the cargo got out. Suppose the sale of the ship's stores will soon take place, and release me. We have nearly saved all, but there will be heavy expenses on them. Very different to Whitburn. They are to have one third of the net proceeds of the stores and half the cargo. Should the sailors bring the dog, don't lose any opportunity of disposing of her.

I told you in yesterday's, the crew is a very bad set of men, even the carpenter."

Mary cradles her children, sheds tears for the losses once again thrust upon them and gives thanks for her beloved husband's safety. Her courage, faith and little else have guided her through these years and, even if she doesn't know it, will through the years to come.

The loss of a ship is like the loss of a loyal friend. The Langley, Neptune and Antaeus saw fewer mishaps while adventuring in the warm southern waters of the Islands. The Benjamin, Ann and Betsey plowing through the cold northern sea, ever watchful of dangers to the east and west, left their beloved Captain much before their time. A new ship must again be found.

Sometime between April and September 14, 1829, Mary delivers a baby boy. He is named Charles, a name that passes down two generations. The only documentation of Charles' birth is a letter of September 29, 1929, when William rejoices that Mary and baby are well.

The Success 1829-1833

The Success, like the Captain's previous vessels, is a brig. The bill of sale is dated the 31st of May, 1830.

It is becoming more difficult, with every year, to make enough money for William to secure a future for his family. Ships from the Baltic are coming into the trade eliminating the need for the British ships to sail to the North. There are offers of freight to be taken to Dublin and Bristol but the Captain is *"unwilling to go any voyage but to London. Ships have been going for £12. I see nothing but starvation here. Insurance for the new ship, approved by the Surveyor will be £1200 at 4&1/2 guineas percent for the remainder of the year, and 10 guineas for the ensuing year. They never do it for less."*

By September 14th Captain William is in South Shields, waiting to load coals. The brig *"is not entirely tight"* and must be caulked before setting sail. He hires 12 men to do the work because it will be less costly than putting her into dock and sinking her to tighten the hull. *"I save 6 a day on each man, besides a foreman's wage and innumerable charges it won't cost, including carpenter's wage for fitting the windlass, etc. £20. It would have been bad policy to have loaded and had to discharge again. Everyone thinks her a good bargain."*

The North Country is suffering. *"There is nothing doing. They want freight and ships want load. A very little time would make the coal owners give a fair rate of freight, would the ships but stand out. Times are tough. George Stephenson's wife's sister's husband has failed, a grocer in North Shields named Dodds."* There is no end to the depressing economic woes.

Finally, September 24th, he is loaded with 14 keels and 3 chaldrons, the measure equal to 16 keels. Life goes on in this fashion, load in the north, sail south, load cargo in London and be off to the north again. William buys and sells. When not sailing he seems to have a finger in many pies whether in Sunderland or Shields or London. The leaks in the ship are not all gone but hopefully they will sail on the night tide.

Each time the Success sails she leaks. Try as they do the leaks cannot be stopped. There is nothing to do but *"sink the ship."* Sitting on board at Coronation Spout, on the River Tyne, Thursday evening, December, 10th, 1829, William writes to Mary and relates the story.

> *"We sunk the ship the night before last, not having time to wait for the day tide and am happy to tell you we found the leak. It proves a trennil hole, bored from the inside nearly 'thro and left so. The water came out in a stream the size of a quill, and when touched with a small nail, burst out a hole an inch and a quarter in diameter. Now, my dear Mary, have I been going voyage after voyage, thinking she was a good ship and would not get worse, when wood not thicker than a biscuit stood between us and sinking.*
>
> *We have lost no time, as had we got loaded last week, should not have gone to sea with such a strong southerly wind as has prevailed for a long time. A ship that had sailed nine days was only as far as Scarbro'. A good many remain and will not sail until a fair opportunity. I am to load a coal much lighter than last voyage and make better out. I am now sleepy, being up the night the ship was sunk, and last night until nearly five o'clock in the morning, and have walked to Newcastle and back today. Good night my darling. I think it long to see you all again."*

The coals proved heavy, not light, creating a greater danger of "*catching the ground*" after leaving the Spout. Loaded with 14 keels and drawing 15 feet of water, in a light NE breeze, for safety sake, they were towed to sea.

Christmas at home is a real treat for William and his family. The Antigua voyages seldom allowed the Captain this special time. 1829 ended on a high note even though the world around them was already showing signs that the winter was to be a bitter one, heralding hardships for so many.

1830

A wickedly, cold January introduces the year 1830. The Success is *"safe moored"* at one of the East India ship buoys, Northfleet Hope It is Tuesday, January 19th, 1830, 9 p.m. By Sunday morning much ice has formed on the water causing some difficulty in boarding and getting underway.

> *"We got underway and got below Woolwich, when Captain Thompson, who acted as Pilot, laid us aground. The next morning, got under sail and into Long Reach, and stopped before the tide was spent in what we considered a good berth for the ice, but contrary to expectation, got a good scouting on the Tide of Ebb, but did not drive today, again not liking the look of the weather, stopped here, for which I am thankful as it blows a strong gale easterly.*
>
> *Wish the Boreas may escape without loss as the two or three days easy weather would tempt the ships at the foot of the river to be getting on and now like Ruffian, is turning on them. We have now very little ice and if it should make stronger the large buoy will entirely break it off from striking the ship with any violence. Although I say thank God that we are no lower down. It will prove a bitter night to many I fear. I shall continue to act with prudence, without regarding any other ship's movements, and doubt not but it will answer the best purpose in the end."*

It was in fact a very bad night but they remained fast to the buoy and the next day William left the ship to go to Gravesend to buy a few pairs of warm stockings.

The winter is fierce. Lonely and cold, William seeks closeness to Mary and so he writes.

> *"The wind and weather still continues very stormy with frost and snow. It pulled a little yesterday, and one ship got towed out. Another put back on the Bar. Serious apprehensions are entertained for her being able to clear land."*

The Captain's Mary

With frozen hands, icy ropes, slippery decks and easterly gales they make their way to South Shields where news of frozen inland waterways has all commerce at a standstill. Ships are not able to get away and if they do every day brings accounts of loss.

> *"The Clubs are terrible, yet they blindly urge the ships to sea and to a constantly glutted market to their ruin. Ship owners seem worse than mad. Man is a discontented, ungrateful animal. I try all I can to be otherwise, and it's sinful to repine at being safe in a good harbour, when so many have suffered at sea. I have my crew at short allowance, and must just wait with patience, a change of weather, and am moored alongside the Planter in the best birth in the harbour."*

A weary captain is loaded with light coals, 14 keels and 5 chaldrons, and ready, when the weather improves, to head for home. He is pleased with the Success.

> *"It is not so deep as any other voyage, labouring through the seas it will not push so much water."*

Through all this, Mary must tend to her own shop, collect money and pay bills. Son William, a very responsible young boy, is a great help to his mother. She is able to send him with messages and rely on the fact that he will do her bidding. The dependable young fellow proudly and efficiently completes his errands.

Despite the reality that the last few voyages have reaped a profit, Mary's shoulders still strain from the load she is carrying. Little Charles is not a strong baby, being very fretful and prone to much sickness. She prays that he will improve and prosper when the warmer weather comes. Having lost one baby she wonders how she will be able go on if this beautiful boy is taken from her?

William tries to encourage his exhausted wife.

> *"My dear love, I do pity you what you have suffered with our son Charley. God's will be done - you have nobly done a mother's part*

by him, yet I still have hopes he's made of good stuff and will bear a good stretch before he breaks."

He tries a lighter note and tells of a visit to Fenham Hall, a Byers property lost to them years before due to the family's support of the Roman Catholic King James.

"A noble hall it is, with a fine park costing ten thousand pounds a year to live in."

Just a bit out of their reach!

Time passes, spring arrives, the economy is still down and shows no sign of improvement. Due to the harshness of the winter the Success is at Riddle's Spout undergoing extensive repairs. The price of coal is down 2 shillings and 6 pence and about a hundred ships unsold. He assures Mary that even though the Baltic and Archangel trade is decreasing he does not wish to leave the coal trade. He finds that *"most of the Solomons are acting on the principle of sticking it out. I must do what seems best."* Life is so uncertain that profit of any kind is entirely unknown. He worries about his little, ailing son and wants desperately to get home safely and quickly. He must get home!

The Captain and his Boys

It is June 15, 1830 and two excited boys, William, now eleven, and Richard, a robust seven, are with their father on the Success for the first time, heading north to South Shields. They have been battered around by a heavy squall but even missing "*10 tons of ballast the ship remained quite stiff*" and didn't miss a beat. It has proven to be a great adventure for the two new sailors. Mother at home frets to hear their news. Finally, a letter!

"Our dear boys are hearty as bucks. Bill has eaten four and a half biscuits and a round of bread, beef, soup, etc., Dick not quite so much, so, my love, you may perceive they are in a thriving way."

They soon know that their father will not tolerate nonsense and vow to do as they are told. They had learned by watching.

"The boy Jack has been sick and ill, partly I think the effects of eating and no work. In comparison, before he was taken ill, I had to beat him to do the most necessary work about the Cabin, and beating he shall not want if he won't do his work etc."

Time is wasting. Anchored at Yarmouth Roads waiting out a strong northeast wind while the crew continue to do repairs the Captain holds his ground and does not venture *to "Abraham's Bosom"* [alias Lowestoft Road]. He would not take chances with his sons on board.

Young sailor Bill writes to his mother and grandmother:

"I am very well, and so is Richard who has felt rather sick, but got better. The dog has got better and so has Jack. Mackerel is seven for a shilling. I like the sea very well and we had a heavy squall, but I didn't mind it. The Mate has stole Mr. Richardson's pen knife. My love to Grandmother. A kiss for my brother and sisters. Dick joins."

Before daylight the wind is fair and they are under way with the boys seriously attending to their own chores. Captain William writes,

"It is not long before the wind turns foul and before dark looked very badly. The Captain reefed and made the ship very snug. It turned out a bad night but having provided against it, the night passed with comparative comfort. Many cannot have found the contrary, as we saw in passing them by. The boys snug in the cot found little of it. They are high spirited fellows who already have good colour in their cheeks."

Mary chuckles as she envisions her boys as they turn the ship into their own playground. Bill, of course, becomes Captain with Dick as his First Mate. The Success rings with happy shouts and laughter as they ward off pirates and swing high and low from the ropes. She knows that the watchful eye of their father will never let the activity get out of hand. Hopefully, the boys will know what *"No!"* means and know enough to stop. It will always be easy to know where they are playing. Dick's boisterous noisiness will make them easy to trace. *"They are a pair of spirited fellows"* are words of comfort from their father. All must be well.

Hoping to be loaded by Saturday, June 26th, they call on Aunt Dorothy but find her not at home, then walk to Tynemouth, get caught in the rain and return to the ship without visiting Tynemouth Castle.

The constant leakage on the passage north prompts William to take the Brig to Sunderland and sink it once again before they start for home. The leaks surely have to stop sometime.

While in Sunderland an encounter with George Stephenson prompts this tale regarding Eliza's inheritance from her late mother.

> *"George Stephenson is still doing nothing, but superintending the repairs of the house. They are not much in a hurry as jobs are scarce. What will come to Elizabeth will be swamped and perhaps as she is now of age, will be expected to find funds to meet the deficiency, as I am sure her part will turn out so. So much for good management."*

There is so much history connected to this coastal area along the North Sea. Centuries of battles against foreign intruders have caused impressive castles, priories and fortifications to be built. A walk to Sunderland to visit Hylton Castle, built in 1400, allows the boys to burn off a lot of energy. Mary can feel the boys' excitement as, armed for war, they become part of the life of the Castle.

She can see them. In the central, ground floor gate passage they bravely stand their ground and hold off the intruders from the sea. Climbing stone stairways to rout out any hidden enemy, in the rooms of the four storey tower, their commanding voices instill fear in many a wary foe. On the second floor they find a kitchen, a pantry and a buttery. A family had really lived here! Their father tells them that the Great Hall, with its walls rising to the ceiling, had been the party room, but to them it becomes an echo chamber. On leaving the castle each boy claims and names two of the carved figures on the top of the turrets that frame the entrance. Questions of how, where and why bombard the Captain. What better way to teach the history of

86

their heritage! By the time they walk back to the Success their father doesn't have to worry about any more mischief that day. Tired boys are quiet boys!

Another day, another walk; this time to a castle at Tynemouth, six miles from the Hylton castle. Here the two young soldiers are primed and ready to never surrender but to protect to the end. The 2000 year history is of little interest to the boys. It had been an Anglo Saxon settlement, an Anglican Monastery, a Royal Castle with an artillery fort for defence, accompanied behind by a well-guarded Medieval Priory. The highlight of this adventure, a stone lighthouse, built in 1775, demands that the boys climb to the top. With lightning speed, never hearing their father's call for care, they find themselves hanging on for dear life to the top of their world. The ship on the horizon might be a pirate ship guided by a one legged captain, heading towards the Success. It is time to call it a day and they vow to ward off any pirate that might be bold enough to invade father's territory.

The next day they visit the Marsdon Rock, a large box like rock one hundred feet long, protruding from the sea. This sea stack of magnesium limestone, with a door like cavity that cuts off about one quarter of its length, is well known to have caused terror for many a seaman. Luckily the tide is low and the boys are able to climb the well-worn stairs created in 1803. Imagination knows no bounds. Father knows all the fun places!

In the nineteenth century everything from the 1600's seems very old. The Captain makes sure, by taking his sons to Derwent Haugh, that they realize just how far coal mining has progressed. Here the 1600 practice of wooden waggon ways, with wooden rails, is still used. These rails run from North Durham, following the River Derwent, to Derwent Haugh. One horse pulls a wagon loaded with two tons of coal from the pit to the shed called a straith. Here the horse is unhitched and the wagon is manually put onto a turntable that dumps the coal down a spout into a Keel boat. The Keel then takes the load down river to waiting seagoing ships. This was serious business but really not too exciting. Dick, especially, had a hard time being good. Even so, their father later tells their mother that *they are a pair of lively, spirited fellows.* That same spirit would ensure that both boys would live to the age of ninety four years, each leaving behind legacies of which to be proud.

Play time is over. The Success has to be sunk again. Hopefully this time the leaks will be fixed. William says again *"indeed I wonder how the ship swam with us."* Both boys helping to scrape and paint the boat have earned a slap from their father for *"dirtying their clothes with paint."*

This is a particularly good time for their Father and his two boys. Bill is a blessing in every way. Dick, a bit of a pet, constantly nudges his Father's elbow for attention allowing little time for the Captain to repine.

It is July 7th and if they load the coals the next day they will be on their way home. School will keep the boys home at summer's end. They now have so much to tell their mother and their friends and so much fodder for new exciting games.

November 9ᵗʰ, 1830

High seas keep the Captain in South Shields again, tired and lonely, trying to convince himself that the ever worsening economic conditions all over Britain have not yet dampened his prospects. He knows he is deceiving himself. If only Mary had been able to come with him this time as every once in a while she has been able to do. The boys had made a lasting favourable impression and he wants Dick to know that one of the old pilots was inquiring for "my noisy little boy."

Mary reads…

> *"Rumour states the country is in a critical state. It's said that the Ministers will not let the King inside the City of Newcastle today. If he doesn't gain access, God beware us. Today's Tyne Mercury says his speech has shook the stability of the funds, and has plunged the nation to the brink of a revolution. Thank God we have the Success and Mother would find me what she cannot allow herself to think me, etc. etc. . . . .*

The English people are suffering much already. An unstable currency will create unthinkable hardships for all. In fact, the King did not dine in the city and the chill of the coming winter was of no comparison to the fear of political turmoil.

Prince George was appointed Prince Regent in 1810 and served as King George IV from 1820 to 1830. He garnered little respect and was unable to inspire national unity. Economic turbulence from 1815 to 1820 and support for radical reform drove masses of people into the streets in support of democracy and republicanism. In 1819, in Manchester, troops had been sent in to control the crowds. Parents feared for the safety of their children. William was always concerned for Mary's safety on her journeys to or from spending time with him.

1831

Over the years the life of a Mariner has not been kind to William's health. Many letters have told of stomach and bowel complaints accompanied by deep depression. In February 1831, Mary is alarmed when she hears of one such severe attack and she begs him to seek medical advice. The letter of February 3, 1831 is a typical male's response.

"After getting on board, feeling myself much better, I took a glass of hot grog and the pain being relieved, I thought myself well and proceeded down the river, but common prudence told me to anchor at Gravesend, but your reproaches still tingling in my ear, I rashly passed the last place where medical assistance could be had, in case of the return of my illness, and ran down to Leigh Flat, and it returned with a vengeance and I suffered dreadfully all night, all Saturday and all Saturday night, until Sunday morning when I took a dose of salts and in the course of the day felt better, but very weak after such a long purging. On Monday morning got anchor weighed at daybreak, wind SW with snow showers, and had to anchor, but, it clearing away again, got under sail and run the Swain and had a good gallop all night.

My favorite anchor stock broke, and put the spare anchor in its place. On Tuesday morning, about eight o'clock, it came on a heavy gale at southeast and the heaviest snow I ever saw in my life all day. At 1 p.m. hove too under the two closed reefed topsails, sea mountains high. The spare anchor washed away. Now, thinks I, the plot thickens. I had fair warning to quit the ship at London by that fit of illness, but would not take it, however, let's play out the play, I can but die. I now pity my wife for her harsh expressions and reproaches to me, and was only anxious to tell you so, however the wind did not get any more on the sand, and the good Success made excellent weather of it but sore did struggle. Never will I call her a tender ship again. One Master told me he had to take every stitch of canvas off the ship, and another that he shifted his ballast. The coast is strewed with wrecks, but I hope rumour makes a bad job worse, with loom or dung for ballast, should assuredly gone to pot. He does pretty well."

London too had one of its fiercest winters. Heavy blasts of wind rattled the windows and crept under the doors. Chimneys howled as stoves, with their low allotment of coal, tried in vain to keep the shivering children well and warm. All four of Mary's coughed, at times, with raging fevers. Bill and Dick had stronger constitutions, and Ann being *"always round and robust"* bounced back quickly. The same could not be said for little Mary and Charles. Mustard plasters worked for Mary but even *"Dr. Ned could not lighten Charles great suffering."*

With a heavy heart Mary writes to her husband, April 15th and says,

"My poor Charles is so unwell that for fear of the worst happening, which God forbid it, think it better you should be prepared. He needs no internal medicine and provided convulsions keep off do not apprehend danger, but he is so much reduced and so extremely cross that I am almost ill myself with want of rest added to a bad cold. He will not go near Eliza without crying, indeed I cannot tell you how distressed I am."

The Success has been stuck on the sands and the Pit Men are on strike and Mary hopes when they get back to work the coal trade will be better. If only her wee son could be the same.

90

The winter wore on but all the prayers in the world could not save her darling little son. Day after day he became weaker and at 2:30 a.m., April 24th, 1831, young Charles quietly passed away.

William learns of his wee son's death when Mary's mother, Elizabeth, writes and begs him to *"bear this great trial with Christian fortitude"*.

"Dear Byers,

It is a painful task for me to tell you that we have lost our poor Charles. The little dear breathed his last at ½ past 2 o'clock this morning. His sufferings were great, indeed, and until Saturday, we had great hopes for him, but from that time he rapidly got weaker. It is a great consolation that everything that possibly could be done for him was tried, but alas in vain. The Almighty thought for to take him to himself, and we must resign him. I hope, my dear Byers, you will endeavour to bear this great trial with Christian fortitude. My dear Mary is at present very poorly, as you may suppose. She grieves much indeed, so do we all. My spirits will not admit to me writing more, but beg you will answer this by return of Post. We have a very sorrowful house. God bless you.

From your affectionate,

Elizabeth Huxtable"

The loss of a second child causes Mary to leave her other children with her mother and find solace in her brother Edward's home, St. Margaret's House, Rochester, Kent. In eleven years she has given birth to six children and, as was common in those times, has sadly lost two.

William is devastated and from the Success, Pelaw Main, tries to comfort his wife.

If they could be together, William believes that they might help each other heal and, to this end, he begs Mary to come by Steam Packet to Newcastle to spend time with him. He needs his best friend just as much as she needs him.

"I cannot be happy until I see you and am certain the feeling is mutual. The pitmen are again on strike leaving men and ships idle

once more. About a dozen pits are at work, having granted the pitmen's demands. Let us again have the happiness of meeting. If the pitmen don't go to work at a reasonable time, my love, you can only go back to the family and business. The country round the ship will afford us nice walks without troubling anyone."

He will meet her on Thursday and adds *"if convenient, bring me cotton drawers and stockings. Also bring a cake of soap."*

So it was that on the London Steamer, the New Edinburg, William said *"damn the money"* and arranged for the price of 2 guineas for Mary to travel with the best accommodations possible. Aware of the danger of gangs in the streets young Bill escorts his mother by Hackney Coach to Blackwell Stairs and then a waterman takes her onboard.

"My love, don't encumber yourself with much luggage. Come in a sort of light marching order and bring tea and coffee with you. I hope Mother will throw no objection in the way. It will disappoint me sadly, and you have to come one voyage this summer, therefore, cannot at a fitter time. It will be the best means of putting you into spirits and allaying your spirits."

The time together works for them and Mary returns home to deal with her loss, comfort her children and her ever loyal mother and get on with her busy life. Being stoical she will stand tall and meet all odds.

School is out for the summer and July 23rd, 1831 finds the boys again with their father, on the Success, in Harwich Harbour. They are now seasoned sailors loving every aspect of their summer life.

"Our kiddies are fine fellows, too much so for the shop keepers, but you will hear enough of their deeds from themselves. Dick has shewed several traits of a kind, good disposition, but is ferocious at times. They quarrel and are kind again. They remind me of their uncles, Jem and Ned."

The summer goes quickly, with no mishaps to recount and too soon, for the boys, it is time for school again.

Another Autumn,
Another Voyage

September 20th finds the Success in Newcastle amid some two hundred sails waiting for coals. Surprisingly the wait is not long so that by October 2nd they are on their way home, encouraged by strong southerly and SE gales.

Even though the weather has moderated the ship has taken in a great deal of water forcing the Captain to dock at the Humber.

> *"However, all that can fetch are come in. Mr. Elliot, of the Salus, tacked and stood out to sea. He has the quarantine flag up. It appears to me that it is no use stopping the holes we find in the ship's bottom as she gets no tighter for it. The crew are very willing, and after getting a little pump leather, are now ready to proceed again. The coals and ballast that comes up the pump destroys the leather as fast as the carpenter can put it on, when a pump is nearly constantly going. Adieu for present, as the ship is not come to anchor. I ought to have been home yesterday. I am always in luck's way."*

A ship flying a quarantine flag sends unimaginable cold fear down every Captain's spine. The fear of cholera or ship's fever, already on the Baltic ships, has so far been only a threat. Knowledge that one of the ships of the United Kingdom is quarantined brings the dreaded disease too close to home. It is a point of honour that any ship's captain is solely responsible to fly the flag when necessary. Harbour Masters must send such vessels away.

Through heavy seas, leaving behind many damaged vessels, the Success arrives home only to set out again in October; this time with Mary on board for the journey north. This enables her to renew her friendship with members of the Byers family and enjoy a time of rest and relaxation with her husband. Loading takes too long so she returns home on another vessel leaving William, docked at Yarmouth, to worry for her safety.

In November, a ship from the Baltic carrying a crew with cholera, docks in Sunderland Harbour. The Port authorities reject it but allow it to dock. An epidemic of cholera in St. Petersburg, in 1823, where more than fifty two thousand had died, has caused the British Government to rule that all ships from the Baltic be quarantined and refused dockage in the United Kingdom. Now with the disease on a British ship fear runs rampant through the hearts of all at sea.

This fear prompts William to say. *"I am anxious to be at home again. Would our circumstances warrant, I could be content never again to leave you?"* The tenacity of the Captain must be admired. November has always brought bitter winds and rough seas; at least when he waited for cargo in Antigua he did not freeze. Even the pesky mosquitoes were better than the icy winter of the north.

Waiting at Wallsend, River Tyne, Nov. 15th, with northwesterly winds causing a strong black frost, a chilled Captain bemoans the fact that the carpenter *"has found so many holes that I wonder how the ship swam. If stopping holes will make a ship tight, ours, ought to be, and, trust, now is"*.

1832

Months go by in a similar pattern. William treks back and forth to the north, Mary keeps everyone's ducks in a row and the children grow like weeds. The summer comes and to the delight of the two girls they are allowed to sail with their father and the boys. Mother is a little apprehensive but knows that even she will benefit from the change of routine. There is just one problem, the promise to write often is not kept. July 6th, 1832, she lets William know just how disappointed she is.

> *"Your long and anxiously looked for letter came safe to hand this morning. I had flattered myself you would be down on Sunday and that I should have news from you on Tuesday, but when Wednesday and Thursday passed without bringing me the wished for information of your safety my uneasiness knew no bounds, and severely did I reproach myself for embarking all my treasures in*

one shipment. Even a merchant who barters for gold would have been more cautious, but no matter, all is well that ends well.

I trust in God my venture will return safe and improved health. I should like to be with you all, but that is impossible. I could very much fancy one of your jaunts and think I see you all very busy. Who is head man of your concern? You didn't tell me whether any one was sick; my poor little Mary, was she frightened?

In short, I am disappointed with your letter, you enter into no particulars all of which would be so interesting to me. I depended on you for more consideration but disappointment is not new to me. I must learn to submit to neglect.

Tell Richard we thought of his birthday, likewise Ann on the 4th of this month. Mary's is on the 24th and William's on the 21st, so they will, I fear, all be passed before your return. God bless them and send them many happy returns."

She is really very lonesome; her house is too quiet and , *"not like home."* She doesn't know just where they are and ends by saying that *"Shield's air is no better for the children than London as it is far more smokey."*

Healthy, tanned sailors return with many a happy tale to tell. Girls can be sailors too!

Later in October at Wallsend, the crew is busy smoking out 11 rats and 13 mice - with no doubt more to come while the Captain puts his pen to paper. Money, as usual is tight, leaving Mary the only option of asking her mother for help. He knows that this will not make her happy. Having dined at sister Dorothy's he is not impressed *"with her single glass of ale. Her husband is not stinted, he may drink a quart if he likes - I got her the chairs without any expense."*

He has found a bit of family history. In trying to determine whether he or Michael Byers was of the older Byers branch he learned that in 1715 his Great Grandfather had been a Captain of the Rebels. In the Jacobite uprising of this time James Francis Edward Stuart (the old Pretender) tried to regain the throne of England, Ireland and Scotland for the exiled House of Stuart.

Crewmen have *"not been stellar"* prompting William to *"engage two young men to be bound 3 or 4 years."* He says *"the Ship is badly manned with the present trash"*.

The following letter dated Success, South Shields, February 27th, 1833 is the last letter written by William to Mary from the North of England. It may have been his last voyage in the coal trade.

"My Dear Mary,

I got safe down from Wallsend last night, wanting three keels. I went to Pearson on Saturday to speak to him about paying the keel dues. He flew into a passion. I kept my cool. But the only point I gained was making him quit his office. I would have thrown up the turn, but had ascertained that it would be an injury to myself. Things I found even worse. The harbour is very full, but have good berth, but, alas, cannot live by laying. I have not spirits to write much. Wrote to George Marshal & Son today to insure one hundred and fifty pounds in the freight etc.

Thursday Morning -- The wind is at SSW, the same as off Scarbro'. I am all out of patience, but a change must soon take place. Charles Thompson was at Newcastle yesterday and was told everything was at a standstill. Could sinful Nature be content, I should not repine, with such a wife, but words cannot express what I feel, and such kiddies.

And again, had I taken at first the 7 shillings and 6 pence, the rat hole would have lost me the ship and perhaps my useless life. The latter I account daily of less value. I have got 'the Reminiscences of Charles Butler, Esq.' educated at Douay College, which, I think, will please Mother and you.

I have nothing more to write about, and should I not write again in three days, conclude we sailed. With love to Mother and bairns, remain, my dear Wife, your ever affectionate Husband,

Your Wm Byers"

The Lure of the Pines

In 1829, Charles Thompson, the Captain's brother-in-law, had sailed to Pictou, Nova Scotia on his ship, the British, and had returned loaded with white pine for the building of ship masts. William had picked his brother-in-law's brain and was intrigued by the news of the growing North American east coast and Quebec timber trade. He could see that British manufactured products and sugar from the Indies could be carried one way with the return voyage bringing forest timber to ease the burden of Britain's disappearing forests.

William began to dream of a new life as a timber baron, owning the forest and building a beautiful home for his family. He was very tired, really bone weary of the long absences from home. He saw no prospect of a prosperous future for his children if they stayed in Britain.

"I have a decision (to make). Either I join the steam trade or take a bigger step and leave my Homeland."

Mary had hinted many times that she wanted an easier life for her industrious boys. He thought again of the mighty forests in Russia and the business built from them and he knew what he wanted to do. His beloved England was letting so many people down. He felt that, he too, should pull up stakes and venture to the beckoning Canadas. To separate Mary from her brothers would be difficult, but they too seemed to be moving on and he knew that where Mary went her mother would go too.

In 1832, ships were daily lining up in England to take emigrants to a hopeful life. Farmers, tradesmen, labourers, people of means with the idea of owning land, and people from all walks of life were leaving weekly. Being one's own master and not being subservient to anyone made it easy for many to make up their minds. Those who could paid for their own passage. Others were sponsored by family or friends who were already settled. Many had nothing but the clothes on their backs. Church of England parishes paid the passages for their paupers and even provided the basic tools to begin life in the new land. These people were some of the most successful. They knew only hard work would gain success. The British Government gave aid to no one, even though the more people who left, the more easily Britain could solve many problems.

Grants of land by the British Government in Upper and Lower Canada were not always fair. The rich were able to acquire large tracts of prime land and leave ordinary colonists with inferior holdings scattered over long distances. This smacked of the Old World patronage from which so many had run already. Too frequently, disheartened new arrivals were disappointed with the dominance of the elite and a depressed economy. It wouldn't be long before this social and political unrest would lead to the rebellion of 1837-1838 and the quest for responsible government.

Why did the Byers Family Leave England?

During 1830 to 1832, Britain came very close to a revolution. Support for Parliamentary Reform reached unprecedented heights. People wanting a better life were in the streets. Political unions were formed. In 1830 the Duke of Wellington's Tory Government was forced to resign when he stated that the people of Britain had full confidence in the unreformed system. This led to widespread rioting throughout the United Kingdom.

The authorities lost control in Derby, Nottingham and Bristol. Castles and country houses of the elite were reinforced against attack. During the winter of 1831-1832 the nation stood on *"a knife edge."* The King recalled the Duke of Wellington to form a government. Reformers were not content and made plans to remove funds from the banks and bring the country to a halt.

Since the end of the Napoleonic Wars, in 1815, Britain had been plunged into a deep economical and agricultural depression. The modernization of industry, and the introduction of weaving and sewing machines had thrown many out of work, leaving them unable to feed their families. Those still working in airless, confined spaces appeared a spiritless and defeated lot. Not until 1833 was a law passed that limited the maximum weekly working hours for adults to 72 and 48 for children. New modern inventions threatened even the chimney sweeps.

By the 1830's the arrival of the threshing machine and other agricultural implements had greatly reduced the number of labourers needed to plant and harvest the crops. Farm workers were often not suited for factory labour. The only hope they had was the news from early immigrants to Upper and Lower Canada who wrote of the opportunities to own and farm one's own land. Prosperity was out there. Many were already leaving and not looking back.

British soldiers, returning from service in the War of 1812, found, like after any other war, that their jobs were gone with no new ones in sight.

These desperate times for the working poor created more slums with garbage and sewage a constant battle to control and with which to live. In 1832 cholera broke out again in East London. Houses were whitewashed with lime and barrels of tar and vinegar were burned in the streets. For most people there was simply no treatment and the inevitable symptoms of diarrhoea, vomiting and sweating were soon followed by death. In addition, the ever present tuberculosis was known to kill even more than did cholera.

Mary and Elizabeth rejoiced when young William won his battle with a terrible winter cold. Fortunately, cholera had not crawled under their door. Captain William with his bowel complaints was a prime candidate for the dreaded disease. Being at sea did not make him safe. Ships under quarantine were still a threat to British seamen.

The north, with its ship-building and coal trades, was not immune to the recession. Mechanization here also resulted in the loss of jobs. Keels and keel men were disappearing. The trusty little keelboat had been a necessary carrier of coal since the wagon ways had been shut down. Now mechanized carts, on steel rails, transported the coal to the spout where it slid down into waiting sea going vessels. Very soon coal fitters and coal trade middlemen would go the way of the keelmen.

The Railway was a real demon in that it obliterated the inland waterway business. NO NEED, NO JOBS! How often the world has seen such progressive dilemmas!

The sailing vessels still transported cargo. Sugar, rum and other manufactured goods had to be transported to the north country and goods such as coal, glassware, earthenware, copper, lime and rope had to reach the larger population in the south. The popularity of steamships was always in William's mind. Time meant money and he was smart enough to know that much of the sailing vessel's work would soon disappear, replaced by faster, steam-powered ships.

A Parliamentary committee's conclusion stated that a sailing ship's profit was negative upon sailing from port. A twelve and a half to fifteen percent return was needed to make a profit. Average wear and tear was 7 1/2%. Few could keep going. The Reciprocity Act of 1824, favoured Prussian and Russian ships, shutting out many British ships that had, for years, traded with the northern part of the continent. Mariners were in great difficulty.

Since the sale of the Fountain Inn in 1816, the financial stability of the Clarkson family had been markedly reduced. Following the deaths of Mary's uncles, George and William Clarkson, the only Clarkson money the family had access to was held by her mother, Elizabeth Clarkson Dudderidge Huxtable. It wasn't a great fortune but it was enough to help her family. Her sons, James and Edward Dudderidge, borrowed heavily from her leaving them always in her debt. Neither man seemed to be able to prosper in his endeavours. Ned, the family surgeon/chemist, seemed often to be in poor health, badly in debt and talking of taking his family to Canada.

With no ability to satisfy his creditors, James is being hounded by the Fire Office, an Insurance Company. Frantically *"making up his papers"* he alerts his mother to the disturbing knowledge that, again, he is not making enough to *"keep his house."*

It became evident that there was little future for the family in now not so jolly Olde Englande. With her three children and their spouses struggling to get ahead, and fifteen grandchildren soon to be seeking their own fortunes in the world, Elizabeth Huxtable knew, deep in her heart, that the family had to leave their island home. She could barely entertain the thought. She would be left alone to die, a broken-hearted old woman with no family to care for her. They, however, would have a chance.

With hushed voices, Mary and the Captain, James and Miriam and Edward and Betsey, met to hammer out a plan. The children must not know and dear Mother could not know just yet.

Their only hope was the Success. It was their means of passage out of England. England desperately needed timber and Canada had the most wonderful timber in endless supply. They would sail to the Port of Quebec, load the Success with squared timber and send her back to London with a hired Captain and crew. The family would stay behind where Captain William intended to become a timber merchant and James and Edward would build a dry goods business in the growing hub of Montreal.

The plan came together very well and the family began to consolidate its resources. James' dry goods business on Fenchurch Street was doomed to failure along with so many other businesses that were going bankrupt at the time. The Byers' Ship's Chandlery business could be sold but it would have to be a quiet deal. The danger was that James' indebtedness to his mother might bleed away the last of the Clarkson money.

It soon became obvious that James and Miriam and their eldest son James (Jem) must stay behind. If there was any inkling that they were about to leave the creditors would swoop down. Living in London was like living under the constant eyes of a vicious flock of predatory birds, each ready to strike and defend their part of the spoils. They would follow later but the younger children would leave with their cousins.

There was so much to do. It could not all be accomplished before the voyage which must happen soon if the best sailing season was to be accessed. There was no time to sell the Dudderidge property at Bridgwater in Somerset and there were business accounts to be settled. Trusted family friends would be left with those tasks.

When the Success sailed in late May, 1833 few realized that the goods being loaded on board were the precious possessions of the Byers and Dudderidge families. It was common to see such activity along the dockyards of the Thames. People were emigrating to North America all the time.

No one noticed that James and Miriam were nowhere to be seen. It grieved Elizabeth that she did not get to say goodbye but she understood.

In a letter, dated May 31, 1833, to his mother, Elizabeth Huxtable *"Passenger on board Success for Montreal,"* James writes,

"My Dear Mother,

Ned will tell you how impolitic it would be for me to leave home. I much feel it and but for this should be fairly off.

I have enclosed 10 Sovereigns and wish it could be more, but you will have no wants that cannot be met with means you have with you be supplied. I hope now all will go smooth and that you will have a pleasant voyage. I should have liked to have been with you, and Jem, on his return, quite regretted he was not going. Mind you live well, wine, beer and grog, at least three times a day, and take care of yourself. Give my love to Mary and the children. Get some of them to write at every opportunity and particularly on the day of arrival, which will be the 7th July. If it should be so, what a prophet I shall prove. Good bye. Miriam desires her love to all, and remain, dear Mother,

Yours affectionately,

James Dudderidge"

The Decision

How did they eventually make up their minds? There was so much darkness on one side of the Atlantic Ocean and so much hope on the other. William's mother, Ann, had passed away but he would leave behind his sister Dorothy and her family. On the other hand Mary, taking all her family, wanted to leave the hopeless life of London.

The Success
(Original oil painting by Mary Byers McNabb; Photo by John Byers)

Their most important asset was the *"Success."* Few people owned their own vessel. They were lucky even if the trusty Brig was a leaky one. It had never let its Captain down.

Whatever the reason, whatever the state of their finances, May 31, 1833, seventeen passengers boarded the Success and sailed from London praying that they would safely reach British North America. It was very, very far away.

At the time of sailing, Captain William was forty-eight years old, Mary forty-two, Elizabeth sixty-five, Eliza was twenty-two, young William fourteen, Ann twelve, Richard ten and little Mary was eight. The others were Ned and Betsy Dudderidge and their children, Maria, Fanny, Elizabeth and James, along with James and Miriam Dudderidge's children, Edward, William and Miriam. James and Miriam's son James stayed with his parents to help them to close down their business.

Each of the seventeen felt the departure in his or her own way. The children were excited about the great sea adventure. The adults, with a mixture of regret and loss of so much each had held dear, knew that only optimism and good will would enable so many of one family to agreeably spend so long a time in such a confined space so far from land.

As a family unit they had never before spent so much time together. The Captain would get to know his family as he had never before. Surely an easier life, without political upheaval, cholera, and failing economic times awaited them. With true optimism they hoped they were not going from the pot into the fire.

On Their Way May 31, 1833

Forty miles down the Thames River from London, perhaps reluctantly and possibly with a few tears, Mary and her mother wave goodbye to Sheerness and the Fountain Inn. The Isle of Sheppey, with its marshy shores, at the mouth of the Thames, had been Mary's get-away, to escape and to dream. She and her mother would never forget the many friends, locals and wanderers from the sea, who had faithfully frequented the old Inn. Many a story of shipwrecks and storms, told by swarthy sea captains and salty sailors would forever be treasured memories. They had loved and were loved and would be missed by many, many friends.

Elizabeth was proud of her daughter. Lessons in relationships and business management had been well inculcated. Mary's ability to successfully operate her retail business and her husband's dealings at the same time as raising a young family, was a true testament to the essentials Elizabeth had instilled and nourished in her daughter.

Tragedy, the deaths of the first Mary and little Charles, and the loss of William's ships to the fierce storms of the North Sea and the Atlantic Ocean bore heavily on both Mary and William. They had, over the years, many times, said that they wanted a better life for their children away from the many hardships of the sea.

Just because the good ship is not laden with coal does not mean it will labour more easily. Each member of the family has stowed away treasures that just could not be left behind. Mary's gift of the dining room table and chairs brought from Antigua, the treasured Georgian desk, the Grandfather Clock, the Christening bowl, the wax doll, books, books, and more books, beautiful shells and so much more found a safe dry place to travel to the vast unknown.

A calm sail down the Thames to the Downs lets everyone settle into the new confines of space but is a false entry into what is to come. Southeast gales fight with the beaten sails, high waves top the bow calling all hands to man stations that will be each one's responsibility for the many weeks to come. For three days the Captain cannot take the Success out to sea. The next dawn is breathtakingly beautiful, and the pilot tows them out.

As the sails unfurl, Mary, now a seasoned sailor, tells of dangers along the coast of Kent bordered by the Thames Estuary and the White Cliffs of Dover. Storms from any direction can drive ships onto shore or onto the shifting sands. The wind has picked up and because it is dangerous she assures the children that their father will find safe anchorage if necessary. She tells stories of ship wrecks on the three mile length of pebbled shore by the *"Needles,"* three triangular stacks of chalk that rise out of the sea, off the western coast of the Isle of Wight.

Northeasterly winds have caused many a wreck. West winds in the narrow, three hundred and fifty mile long English Channel, joining the North Sea and the Atlantic Ocean, can quickly land ships in Calais, France, or anywhere on the western coast of Europe. Dangers abound. The children trust that their father knows what he is doing and there will be no such happenings.

It is a long trek around the southern coast of England with the winds seeming to say *"Stay, this is your home, turn around, come back."* Nature seems to do all it can to hold them back. Cognizant of the challenge before him, the Captain opts to dock for a final safety check of the Brig's contents and loved ones. He indeed has all his eggs in one basket. After two days in Portsmouth they turn their backs and set out to sea. Two weeks from when they left home they can see no land; they are really on their way.

With no mishaps, following time worn British trade routes and mindful of currents and Trade Winds, the Atlantic Ocean becomes their summer home. Home is home; meals have to be prepared and dishes washed and put away. This along with daily tidying up keeps the three girls busy. The boys, old seasoned sailors that they are, proudly show off their skills. They know what to do and, most certainly, they know what not to do.

Through fair winds, summer storms and the too frequent *"Trade Winds on holiday"* the Captain praises his First Mate. *"Well done Mary"* is a constant call. Over the years, while on long voyages, he had been known, many times, to tell his First Mate that the man's skill did not compare to those of his dear Mary.

A month later a tanned crew sails south of Newfoundland and towards the much touted forests of Nova Scotia. Charles Thompson had not exaggerated; the land is beautiful, the pines breathtaking. It is so good to set foot on solid ground, top up supplies and meet new people in Pictou. Mary shared the energy of her husband but the stay seemed too long making Mary fearful that William might want to stay and not go on. She wants to be much farther inland away from the sea. Thankfully William finally agrees and the good ship Success takes them on their way.

Along the rugged coastline, heading north, they conquer the challenges of the tides, and enter the confines of the Gulf of St. Lawrence. The world of big water is behind them. They are safe; all being proud of a challenge having been well met.

There is still a long way to go but they are thankfully in reach of land. There is so much to see in the water and on the shore. They have seen whales at a distance but now they can get a better look and they sail along with them. Cries of delight herald the tableau of seals basking in the sun on the rocky shores of the mighty Saint Lawrence.

As they sail on through beautiful, clear, green waters, under heavens free of clouds, the breathtaking tableau of the majestic Laurentians, vibrant with its palette of summer colours, screams *"WELCOME TO YOUR NEW WORLD"*.

In a relaxed atmosphere with wide eyed wonderment, all, not only the children, soon spot deer, moose and bears. In the distance large fish turn over and birds, they have never seen before, find food by skimming over the water while others sing in the marshes or soar to loftier heights.

The History of this New Land

Lower Canada since the time of Cartier and Champlain has been home to fishermen, farmers and fur trappers. As the Success makes its way, tidy settlements nestled along narrow swaths of land along the shores, afford opportunities to dock again and meet more people. The fur trade had brought both the French and the English to these shores so that language is not often a problem.

Their first stop on the south shore is Rimouski. It is a well built up area, settled in 1689, that gives truth to the fact that people do well in this new land. They are much in need of water, food and conversation. The people are friendly and invite them to stay a few days.

Tadoussac, at the mouth of the Saguenay River, settled also in the 1600s, is home to the first Trading Post. Here they stay much longer, adding more necessities, repairing and cleaning the Brig, and doing simple things such as laundry and bathing in the clean, clear water. The river is rich with salmon, an appreciated treat for all. Salmon, seals and whales come this far up the river affording pleasant entertainment for the new visitors.

To accommodate people of means in the 1830s wealthy English and French families had built villas similar to those they had left behind in Margate. Trois Pistoles and Riviere-du-Loup, whaling ports since the seventeenth century, had grown into bustling villages. The adults are heartened by the vista of prosperity they see before them. They are, indeed, sailing with optimism with the whales. Surely all will go well for them. Surely hardship has been left behind.

Based on James' letter of May 31st, with the projected date of arrival of July 7, they should have been in Quebec City by now. Why weren't they?

There are three theories. One is that the Captain perhaps considered staying in this area to take advantage of the unending forest and spent time considering his options.

The second is that all vessels were required to stop and report at an island 48 km. down river from Quebec City. Since 1832 Grosse Ile was a quarantine station to protect Quebec City from immigrants carrying cholera and small pox. Here those contaminated were required to remain a month or until the quarantine could be lifted. There is no evidence, written or legend, that the Success ever stayed at this island.

The third is more probable. The Success had a reputation of being a leaker. Perhaps the Captain had to 'sink it' in Nova Scotia or along the St. Lawrence to find those leaks and fix them before going on.

Quebec City at Last

The Success, and its crew, must look its best for the docking in Quebec City. Proudly her sails must reflect nature's light, ropes must be properly coiled and decks must shine. The Captain, too, Master Mariner that he is, must, in fresh uniform, guide his faithful Brig to its berth.

As they approach the dock they have a quiet time. Time to reflect on the enormity of the mission that they have successfully accomplished.

With great anticipation, they quietly, with the skill of their beloved Captain, throw the ropes and dock. It is September 8th, 1833. The Brig Success has safely brought the Byers Family to make a new home in Canada

The Port of Quebec is a bustling hive of activity nestled snugly below the Citadel which towers over the city. From the water it appears to be an enchanting place but a closer look reveals the tell-tale smells and sights of the port cities of England.

Across the mighty St. Lawrence River from the city sits the smaller community of New Liverpool. Several English vessels are clustered about a large basin where vast rafts of timber are waiting to be loaded onto ships bound for Britain. The Captain is fascinated by the amazing collections of squared timber, floating in the water.

While Mary, Ned and Betsey seek out temporary living quarters for the family in Quebec City, Captain William hires a Canadien to take him over to the south shore where he is introduced to Robert Hamilton of Hamilton Brothers, a company whose headquarters are far to the west at a place called Hawkesbury. Hamilton boasts of fortunes to be made from the vast expanses of timber along the tributaries of the great Ottawa River.

Here the treasured white pine is harvested, an endless supply he claims. The logs are floated down the tributaries to the Ottawa, collected in booms and transported to their Hawkesbury mills where they are squared into the impressive timber floating in abundance at New Liverpool.

Hamilton brags that their Hawkesbury sawmills are the largest and finest in the British Empire. He speaks of the pilots and crews who bring these vast rafts of timber by water to Montreal where the Ottawa meets the mighty St. Lawrence River, eventually travelling with their precious cargo all the way to Quebec City.

The Captain soon has a deal made to quickly load the Success with Hamilton Brothers' timber destined for England. It must all be done swiftly so that the Success can clear the St. Lawrence before winter.

It was the first time Hamilton has met a ship's captain who has brought his whole family with him. It is even more fascinating that this wind-tanned sea dog intends to stay and engage in the timber trade. He must know more! An invitation is quickly extended for dinner the following evening at the Hamilton's Quebec City home.

What an exciting turn of events. It is obvious that the Hamilton's are people of means, an integral part of Quebec City society. Mary flies into action making herself ready for her first social event in her new homeland.

With great excitement, Mary and the Captain arrive at the Hamilton's mansion precisely at the appointed hour. They are ushered in to the front parlour where Robert Hamilton greets them most graciously. His beautiful wife, Isabella, joins them momentarily and immediately reaches out to Mary with warmth and hospitality.

Over a beautiful meal, impeccably prepared and served by the household staff, the Hamilton's regale their guests with tales of life and opportunity in the Canadas. By the time the evening has drawn to an end, Captain William and Mary are convinced that their life in Canada must be centred around timber and the mighty forests in the Laurentian hills.

With Isabella Hamilton's help suitable temporary accommodations are secured in the city and it is time to begin the journey on to Montreal and the land of the white pine.

Within days the Success is loaded with timber and sailing out from the cove at New Liverpool, headed for England, under the direction of a hired captain and crew.

Montreal, September, 1833

Within days Captain William and Mary, Ned, Betsey and Maria are on their way to Montreal by steamer to secure winter accommodations.

By this time, to Mary, a harbour is a harbour and a dock is a dock. Very quickly she sees that Montreal is a *"much superior place to Quebec"*. In a letter from the British Coffee House in Montreal, to her mother in Quebec, she brings her family up to date.

"You no doubt think it long before you hear from me but as I could give no satisfactory account sooner, thought it better not to write. We have taken part of this house, which being convenient to the water and markets, also the most eligible in every respect, think and trust you will be pleased with it as a make shift for the winter. I long to see you all. Have been quite dull & low spirited several times & the goods not arriving as expected quite disappointed us. We are to give eight dollars a month for the lodging from which you command a view of the river, wharves, etc.

Betsey will write by the conveyance. We had a walk together this morning. She is well, also Maria, who wishes for Anne very much. The steamboats outdo ours in England. There is every comfort on board them even to abundance. The ladies, in my opinion, dress rather too much for the occasion but, as it is the custom, we must do as our neighbours do. We shall come back to you as soon as we can get things to right after they arrive, if possible the same day, but at all events the day after, for I shall have no ease 'till you are all safe here. Hope they are all good children. The weather is very fine here. This is a much superior place to Quebec.

Byers says it will take us more than two days to take the furniture, etc., out & may be that they will deliver the salt and other goods first, therefore do not expect us too soon for that will only make you uneasy. Byers joins me in love, etc., to you all."

While Mary puts a winter home together William begins to scout for land. He wants hardwood bush with ample space for farming. West along the

Ottawa River seems to be the direction to go. Land is for sale in Argenteuil County, Quebec. The tiny communities of Grenville, Brown's Mills (Brownsburg), Carillon and St. Andrews are active participants in the timber trade. He feels called to this area.

British military engineers, brought in after the War of 1812, have overseen the building of canals to circumvent the thirteen miles of the Long Sault Rapids along the Ottawa River. Logs could handle the Rapids, people could not. Without the canals the portage had been long and difficult.

The Grenville Canal, started in 1819 and completed in 1833, was a major factor in the growth and development of the vibrant Grenville Village. From 1826 to 1830 the community had established a General Store, a Post Office and a School.

The Carillon Canal, built between 1830 to 1833 on the north side of the Ottawa River and the Chute-a-Blondeau Canal, 1818, on the south shore were built to open commercial and forestry travel from Montreal to Ottawa and beyond. Both are one lock stations with barracks that welcome weary travellers.

A well-established Scottish community, St. Andrews, located on the North River, has a military barracks, a Post Office, and since 1802 a Grist Mill, a Saw Mill and Canada's first Paper Mill.

These communities, along with an Anglican Church, established in 1819, the first in Lower Canada, tell William that he is heading in the right direction.

The autumn of 1833, with all its vibrant autumn colours, speeds by with Mary and family living at the British Coffee House in Montreal and William living with a Mr. Query at Chatham and scouting for land along the flank of the Laurentian Hills. An early snow transforms the landscape into a fairy tale wonderland that, to William, surpasses any other vista he has ever seen. He has plans for the house that he and Mary will build together and is most anxious to put uncertainty behind him.

The Captain's Mary

By December 4th, he buys a snow covered parcel of land, 600 acres in three 200 acre parcels in the rear of Chatham Township, west of Brown's Mills on the edge of the Laurentian Mountains. Although the snow is hampering a survey he is confident that he has made a good choice. He has placed his faith in the advice of local people. He is lonesome and writes to Mary to assure her that money she has sent has arrived safely.

> *"I received your letter by sending Query for it on horseback, say 16 miles. It's such a roundabout road to Carrio (Carillon) thro' the woods. The distance is only 6 miles and a road is making. The money came safe and it is the only mode of sending it. So do understand, it's not to expect letters from me in a regular way or me yours. For instance, I found three of yours at St. Andrew's to care of Brown and Query brought me two.*

> *I am waiting proposals from two different men about building the house and have employed a hunter man to look for the boundaries and expect him in a minute. A regular survey from Brown's Mill is not to be thought of at this season. Everything I hear is in favour of my bargain. They tell me a fine small river runs through No. 24 with a mill site. Perhaps our honest Bill would like to have a mill. The house will be a frame one.*

> *I am getting strong, but have been very ill. I am just told there is a house and clearance on 24 and that the man named Blair has gone to see Mrs. Robinson - it's said he paid part of the money. However, it doesn't concern us, I have not time to say more.*

> *I have no wafers. They will put one on it at the Post Office. Write often. I will be home to you as soon as I can."*

By February, 1834, William is still on the mountain and Mary is in Montreal. It is taking much too long to get the family settled. Eliza has been more fortunate. She is happy and working for Mrs. de Hertel in St. Andrew's. This is a great load off her father's shoulders. His twenty two year old daughter needs a life of her own.

Even though the Antigua voyages and the coal trade had taught William to be patient he is again frustrated.

> *"All Saturday it rained heavy, which stopped Query for going for our land surveying man, and am sorry to say it's thought he is not at home and no man at this season can do it like himself. The woods, owing to the snow, are nearly impassable, should it come a strong frost after the rain. We hope the snow will carry us. Query goes for him tomorrow morning if possible.*
>
> *Query has gone and his boys made us snowshoes, simply pieces of deal board tied under the feet and a devil of a journey we had. I first wished myself back again, being at times up to the middle, the oldest boy and myself alternating pulling each other out. Little Sambo danced around us, but in his capers, after we got to the lake he, broke one of his snowshoes and suffered enough on the way back. The sweat poured off me, but was amply rewarded on reaching the lake. (Half Moon Lake). It would be considered most beautiful in England. It's about two miles. It appears to me that too much water is on the lots after. The lot Query is on is No. 24 and on a careful survey I find ample room for ourselves and effects. I had no notion there was any way near so much, and under all our circumstances duly considered, must make the best bargain I can with Query, and in the summer when the ground can be seen, if we think it fit to build on another situation we can do so. Depend it requires all the lookout possible to decide on before the three weeks allowed expires, but must wait 'til the snow hardens to travel on."*

Query upon his return gives a *"different account of the lake and lands"* and prompts William to *"suspend my intention of making a bargain with Query until I see farther."* He is *"sick of perplexities"* and decides to go to St. Andrew's and Carillon the next day. The last trip to Carillon by train had enabled him to pick up some of his clothes and box no. 2 of books. Slowly the Byers' treasures are coming to their new home.

The Georgian Desk - A family treasure brought from England (Photo by John Byers)

The next day he leaves Query's at 7 a.m. and walks to Carillon, gets there at 11 a.m. and goes to see Eliza. She tells her father that she had been told to tell him "*not to take McArthur's farm as a gift and that Hertel's is not much better.*" Too many opinions! On the bright side he finds that Eliza has nothing to complain about and thankfully four more boxes of books have safely arrived.

Ned in Montreal

Adding to Ned's current 1830 debt of £1200 sterling, his mother, Elizabeth, again lends him money to buy a home, Melvina Cottage, on St. Antoine Street in Montreal. With more of her money, twelve hundred and seventy pounds, nineteen shillings and eight pence he goes into partnership with a Mr. Pring in a large store on Notre Dame Street. "*It is now fitting up and will be the most handsome retail store in Montreal.*"

The Move to The Mountain

With cholera rampant in Montreal living conditions are worrisome. The city is overcrowded and sanitation is primitive. It is too much like the problems they left behind in London. For the health and safety of the family

William accepts Query's offer of a log house and by May 24, 1834 William and Mary's family is on the mountain. Grandmother Elizabeth later describes her move as *"being banished to the bush"*.

Lots 20 and 23 in the 7th Range of Chatham Township and Lot 24 in the 8th Range are now the new wilderness home for the Byers family.

Mary's brothers' families remain in Montreal. A letter to Elizabeth from her grandson James Edward Dudderidge tells that he has been ill, probably with small pox as he says that *"he is getting better looking in the face"*. His father, James, his mother, Miriam and his brother will leave England the first of May on the Joseph Story, having already sent some of their household goods on the Success. His father is to work with his brother Ned in the store on Notre Dame Street. It all sounds hopeful.

Spring on The Mountain

Rains wash away the winter snows and William finds to his dismay that his property is not as he had envisioned. The flat land that is to be farmed, about 200 acres in all, is promising but on the steep hills thin soil and numerous bogs present a challenge that only stout hearts might conquer. The mighty towering white pines are the only signs of hope.

William had never backed away from a difficult situation before and he had no intention of doing so now. Again he learns just how well Mary has raised his children, especially the boys, while he had been away at sea. The two lads shirk no duty. With their father they fell trees and clear land for the house and garden. It is back breaking work but it does not keep Mary and the girls from doing their part. They buy a cow and hens to provide milk and eggs for their table and learn the art of planting and caring for a vegetable garden. They are busy, many times bone tired but they are all together and are building their dream. William is stronger than he had been while at sea but he still has worrisome bowel problems and tends to tire more easily than he would like.

The survey has shown them just how vast their land is. The lake, beyond their property border, now known as Half Moon Lake, provides a place to unwind. The young people need some fun time and soon realize that how fishing and swimming can help to put their young lives in perspective.

Trips by train to Montreal bring back essential household goods and allow a visit with extended family. The cousins are often sent to the mountain for Aunt Mary's care. As in any era, there is the belief that there is always food on the farm and two or three more children cannot possibly be a problem.

All on Canadian Soil

June 23, 1834, on the Ship Catherine, James Dudderidge, his wife Miriam and son Jem arrive safely in Quebec City. They settle in Montreal but Mary's brother James is not well and dies shortly after he arrives. He leaves behind his wife Miriam and his children, James Edward, Edward, Richard, William, and Miriam. Shortly after her husband's death, Miriam gave birth to a son, George.

Cholera had travelled with James. Ned who had been, over the years, frequently ill with breathing problems passes away on August 26th within six weeks of his brother's death. He left behind his wife Elizabeth, better known as Betsey, and his children Maria, Fanny, Elizabeth, Edward, and James.

Monumental Problems for Mother Elizabeth

Who will carry the responsibility for twelve orphaned children in this new world? Elizabeth Huxtable has always helped her sons when times were rough. How will she cope with her daughters-in-law? She doubts that they know the state of their husbands' finances, especially of their debts to their mother.

The business venture in Montreal is now in trouble. Not surprisingly Elizabeth's two daughters-in-law charge James Edward, Miriam's son, the eldest of the Dudderidge children, with the task of getting money from grandmother Elizabeth Huxtable. There is only one problem. The two women have forgotten or are choosing to ignore the fact that their husbands have already received all the money that is legally coming to them and that they are both much in debt to their benefactor. But they try anyway. This is a problem that will haunt Mary and her mother for years.

On August 27th, James Edward writes to his grandmother,

"By this time Aunt (Betsey) must have told you of my dear Uncle's (Ned) death, which I communicated the morning after it happened. You can judge of our state of mind and affliction, and may God give you strength of mind to bear yours with Christian-like resignation.

At present, we are at a complete standstill and it mostly, in fact altogether, waits your sanction to proceed. You are aware of the nature of the funds intended by our two dear relatives to carry on the projected establishment, part a portion of the bond paid by my dear father to you.

We now stand in this position. If you do not wish the above mentioned capitals to be employed in it, we must give it up, and thereby we lose £500 or probably more in relinquishing the concern. You must know the amount my poor father [James] has left barely exceeding £400. You can easily calculate the amount of my poor Uncle's property and again how little their widows can afford to lose a claim so great in comparison with their all.

My dear Grandmother, don't suppose for a moment I would persuade you to do anything contrary to your inclination.

The concern met the approbation of both our dear and best friends. God, who took them promises in his infinite mercy, will never forsake the widow and the orphan, and will give me strength and will to take upon myself the burden they would have borne had it pleased God to spare them. You know Mr. Pring and also my father

(James) and uncle's (Ned) opinion of him. He will carry on the establishment and be the head of it, which was the last wish of my Uncle Ned, written two days before he died, that should he die and his wife (Betsey) wish it to be carried on, he was sure Mr. Pring would do his best for his own and my poor father's children.

I now lay before you the state in which we stand for your consideration. I have no doubt of the success of the establishment. The first men in Montreal say it cannot do otherwise, if well managed. You see the awful responsibility I have incumbent on me, and I hope know me too well to doubt a moment of my thought change. As the strictest attention and constant application will go, it shall have it from me. I trust I am now sober. I feel myself quite a different being and for the future will both think and act as a man. Thank God I am of that age to be able to take upon myself the places of our lost relatives, and believe me while I have life I will work for, protect and succor my orphan cousins, brothers and sisters and any portion of the afflicted family as may require my aid.

My aunt (Betsey) and mother (Miriam) join me in the best love to you all. They would write but are not able. We are all as well as can be expected.

Pray don't decide hastily. You see what rests on your decision. Both mother (Miriam) and aunt (Betsey) are anxious about as may easily be supposed, as ruin almost stares them in the face of your refusal."

What an incredible burden has been thrust upon the aging Elizabeth in her banishment in the wilderness. Her heart, aching with sorrow, is breaking. It is almost too much for her to bear, but bear this tragic challenge she must.

One can only guess what William and Mary's reaction to this letter would have been. The remainder of Elizabeth's money, still to come from settlement of properties in England, is to be given to Mary. William has watched, too many times, the flow of money to keep the brothers afloat. As time passes Mary will be plagued for years by the demands of her two sisters-in-law.

And yet, she understands their desperation…

Grandmother does not come through as expected; in fact it is years before Elizabeth finally completes her business with the notorious Mr. Pring and her Montreal family.

James Edward tries again.

> *"He [Mr. Pring] is no man to treat my poor afflicted mother [Miriam] and orphan family in the manner he has, to cast us adrift. This is the man who professed such friendship for our dear departed relatives and met my mother at the steamer and nearly wrung her hand off (though he had not seen her above three times before) who now that a little difficulty presents itself, he casts us off and we may go to perdition or anywhere else. Pring has told Cuvillier our position at home, and very likely to a dozen more, and also that the last parcel of goods was my father's (James). They are gone to a dead certainty."*

His grandmother is too good a business woman to be taken in by tears and the likes of Mr. Pring. Not so her sons; they had signed no document or articles of partnership clearing the heirs of any responsibilities.

One more appeal for money is made. It will not be the last.

> *"I am terribly in want of money and must have some from my aunt (Mary). At present we are (living) with an old friend, Mr. Hodges, from the Minories in London. He charges £3 per week for all. Upon calculation, I find we could not board ourselves for less and therefore moved here. My mother (Miriam) is very low and nerveless and I think she is amused with the company and the bustle that is here."*

This also didn't work so Miriam has a try at her mother-in-law creating a long standing rift with Mary.

> *"I cannot myself believe that you can wish the representative of your dear son to come up the country and chop wood, while a*

perfect stranger is to have the benefit of that money my dear, dear husband was persuaded for, and half destroyed him."

She goes on to say that she has not been well since her confinement (the birth of George) and can gain no strength by being kept in *"a constant state of agitation not knowing how to act or what your sentiments are now towards us. If I can judge what they might be, by Mrs. D's behaviour, since her return, I should imagine they were hostile for she will not let me have any mourning or money."*

She does not have a penny in her pocket. She feels that *"they might have starved if it had not been for Mr. Hodges and that if they had stayed in their old house in a most unhealthy part of Montreal none of them would have survived."*

Miriam did win and with Elizabeth's money buys property and builds a house on the mountain. She *"has no objection to the bush"* and lands on her feet just down the road from William and Mary.

Miriam wins again and Elizabeth goes to Montreal to settle the mess her sons have created for themselves. This does not prove to be an easy job and prompts some advice from Mary.

October 26th. Mary urges her Mother to sustain any losses she must, knowing it was not of her doing.

"You, my dear Mother, gave up all to support the credit of my beloved, my ever regretted brothers. Now let a fair division of what remains to you be made without favour to anyone. Thus, you will secure to yourself for the rest of your days that tranquillity which a just performance of our duty brings with it. It is snowing pretty fast. I wish it would set in and make the roads at once. You would come down much better than by water."

December 25th, 1834

Christmas on the Mountain will remain in Mary's memory as a blessed family time. Under a canopy of snow covered pines the children revelled in all that a winter wonderland can give. They were together and warm, making new traditions that they thought would carry through many, many years. Sitting around the fire Mary and William dreamed some more, relishing their closeness and the beauty of their active children.

Wrapped in love, the family sees 1834 out and 1835 in.

1835

The Canadian winter sets in with a vengeance. High winds buffet the small log cabin and barn. Snowbanks and drifting winds soon isolate the small communities north of the Ottawa River. Cabin fever is not a stranger in many homes. Thoughts of the new house to be built in the spring inspire many of their family conversations. The young people are kept busy chopping wood and seeing that the woodbox is always full. The steep hills echo with laughter as homemade sleds carry well bundled adventurers down the slopes. Hope, faith and hard work carry them through to spring.

The New House
Woodland Cottage

An agreement between Captain William Byers and Donald McKercher concerning the building of a house on Lot 20, 7th Range, Chatham is signed on January 15th 1835.

> *"I hereby agree to build a house for William Byers thirty six feet long and thirty feet wide to be built in the same manner as Brown's house on the Chute Road, to say log frame house, to be boarded and shingled. The gabled ends to be boarded and clapboarded with a door at one end and a window at the other, and let it be understood, it means in this agreement only spaces for the doors and windows, viz. four windows in the attics and two doors and*

eight windows on the lower floor making a height of four feet in the attic; the beams to be 7 by 8 inches; the rafters to be on the square with Collar Beams; spaces for two chimneys to be five feet wide with a stoop and gallery 7 feet wide the length of the house, doing the creepers and roof, and to be studded & upper beams run out 7 feet, all beams to be planed and headed, except collar beams & sleepers, to find the boards & shingles & nails and to victual himself and all he employs. House to be built as follows: Cedar sills & above ash, spruce and hemlock, the plates to be ash and the beams to be spruce. The sleepers to be ash and hewed on one side, running out 7 feet to form a stoop, rafters to be spruce and balsam mixed.

The agreement to be completed by the first of May for the sum of 36 pounds currency. House to be built on blocks so as to afford height of two feet, stone mason work underneath, on Lot 20, 7th Range, Chatham.

Signed: Donald McKercher, William Byers, Duncan Graham Agreement January 21st, 1835 "

"I hereby agree to furnish eight window sashes and frames, each containing 24 panes to be made Canadian fashion to open sideways for the sum of ten shillings each, and four windows for the attics, each twelve panes to slide up with frames, for the sum of 6 shillings each, and one for the gable end, the same size and rate and to deliver them on the promises free of all expense.

Signed   Allan Cameron
William Byers "

February 10th, 1835

"I agree to dig a cellar for William Byers a yard and a half deep below the surface of the earth, eight yards square for the sum of five pounds, also to square the House timber on all sides for the additional sum of forty five shillings currency. In case of coming to solid rock the cellar bargain to be void paying for the number of yards done.

Signed: Donald McKercher
William Byers

Received the five pounds for digging the cellar.

Signed: Donald McKercher   William Byers
Witness: James Edward Dudderidge"

Woodland Cottage - The House on the Mountain
(Byers family collection)

124

The End of a Dream

Spring 1835 comes with its cleansing rains. Snow disappears leaving creeks overflowing as they hurry down the rocky slopes. All around buds are bursting and spring flowers poke their heads through the fallen leaves of autumn and the cracks of smooth faced rocks. The farm animals kick their heels to limber their limbs and shake off the feel of winter. Young and old soak up the warm sun and plan another planting season.

Money is needed to finish building the house and to expand the timber trade. The boys have ideas that they want to see carried out. The Captain's children have so far done him proud. He knows that his decision to leave the sea has been a good one.

Perhaps all is well in this new spring and perhaps it is not. Over the years Mary's beloved Captain has been plagued by stomach and bowel complaints. Perhaps he has not had a good winter, perhaps a winter grippe has weakened his system. Cholera is rampant in Montreal and following a visit to city, Captain William becomes violently ill and soon dies of the dreaded plague. He is buried on the mountain and many years later his remains are moved to Hillside Cemetery, West Hawkesbury, Ontario, where one can find memorials to William and Mary, side by side on the top of a shady, wooded hill.

A letter written by Elizabeth, Mary's mother, marks the date for history.

> *"Mr. Byers has been in an ill state for some time, for the last six weeks scarcely out of his room and as it has pleased the Almighty to deprive me of my two dear sons who died within six weeks of each other and on the 23rd of June last my daughter likewise lost her husband."*

William has passed away! The unthinkable devastates Mary and her family. Their ship has lost its rudder! They are trapped on the mountain in the Canadian wilderness.

Life Must Go On

A black cloud has fallen on the mountain! Only Mary has the answers; if the times will allow a woman her free will to proceed in a man's world.

Mary has no choice but to continue what she and William have started. The house will be finished and they will carry on… somehow.

A letter to Mary from George Brown, Brown's Mills, Lower Canada (now Brownsburg), shows that she did just that.

July 19, 1835

"Antoine Portreau, the carpenter, is now here present and I have come to an agreement with him to lay your floors in a workman-like manner viz: - the under floor one half to be laid with narrow plank or more if wanted; the upper floor to be planed on both sides - for a consideration of thirty two dollars and to be boarded - and subsisting money must be advanced to support his family as work goes on - and he is to commence on or about the 28 inst. What other work you have to do, the value of which can be more easily ascertained afterwards. Perhaps it may be necessary to mention (to) your masons not to use any more plank than what is actually needful for their scaffolds as whatever they make use of will not be of any use whatever in carpenter work.

I expect your iron to be at the Chute on Thursday from Montreal.

With best respects to Mrs. Huxtable, I am your most obedient servant,

Geo. Brown"

Uncertain Times

Lower Canada in the 1830's is in a period of widespread economic distress fueled by an agricultural crisis that brings many to the verge of starvation. There are people wanting to work but needing immediate money in payment. Will Mary be able to fill this need?

Thus begins the heartbreaking task of getting money from England. Elizabeth and Mary soon find that trustworthy friends can let you down. They have money, they just have to get it. Lawyers Hunt, Anderson, Neate and Fitzgerald & Son procrastinate, withhold or even spend the money for years. Letters and promises cross the ocean to no avail. Had it not been for Mary's childhood friend, John Hunt, the money might never have materialized at all. The sisters-in-law, especially Betsey, cloud the waters constantly, even by going to England in search of a solution. When they remarry it is even worse as the new partners smell money leaving no stone unturned. It takes almost ten years, at times near starvation, to finally win the battle.

There is no end to Mary's problem. She knows that she must sell some of their possessions and feels certain that some of their books will sell easily but hates to sell the animals. If she does how would they live? To make matters worse her creditors are demanding payment for agreements that had been honourably signed. She soon finds that people just do not have money to spare and is offended when told, *"you are not, however after all, the object of philanthropic sympathy. It is not so very bad to be dependent on one's mother. It is far more unpleasant to live on the forbearance of strangers."*

July 18, 1835

Work on the house has progressed to the point where the floors are to be laid. Mary's agreement, already signed, means that the carpenters can go ahead without any delay. This gives the family real hope that they will soon be under their new roof. New energy is found to tend the garden and fields, future food for the family and their precious animals. The fall harvest gives promise for the long months of winter.

1836

One thing bothers Mary. William has been gone for some time. Why has she heard nothing from his family back home? Surely his sister Dorothy would wonder how her brother's children are coping without him. Surely there could be some way for them to help, even perhaps by helping to straighten out the silent lawyers that frustrate her and her elderly mother. Relationships are tense between Mary and her sisters-in-law but they are not estranged. Deep in her heart she knows that they, too, are trying to find a way to the future for their children.

The hard, cold truth is that widows were fair game in the society of the day. They were expected to quickly re-marry and live under the protection of their new husbands. Some men, unscrupulous sorts, feel entitled to take advantage of poor widows. Mary know this and she knows that her isolation in the Canadian wilderness will not serve her well. While some might have accepted defeat, her unfortunate reality steeled her resolve and re-doubled her determination to seek justice for her children.

As if thinking of something conjures it up, out of the blue a letter, a kind letter, dated June 26, 1836 arrives from William's cousin, Michael Byers of Sunderland. She had written to him the previous August telling him of William's death. Twice he had come to Montreal on his ship Earus since they had left London but said that he could not find a trace of them and hadn't written because *"he did not know whether a letter by the Post in the winter season would reach them and should certainly have made every endeavour to have seen you, but thinking you had gone to Upper Canada where I should have little or no chance of finding you in such a wilderness of a country. I form but an indifferent idea (of) traveling in Canada from the little knowledge I have of it."* He would like to see her and asks that she send him specific directions.

Just hearing from a family member from her old home gives Mary a bit of hope, her spirits lift and her heart seems lighter. Surely now she will hear from Dorothy! She doesn't and things get worse.

The fair summer didn't mean a good year. The weather changed, too much heat and then devastating rains that ruined garden and field crops. There is little money earned and no money from England. Elizabeth, in desperation, writes to Mary's friend, John Hunt in England.

> *"At present the property you hold of mine is entirely independent of anyone as when I left England not an individual on earth had any claim on me, not even for as much as a single shilling, and under all circumstances I must say that I have been very unfairly dealt with, but where the fault rests, I do not know. But it is to you, sir that I must seek for redress."*

She knows the Sheerness business is settled and wants the three hundred pounds remitted to her. She goes on.

> *"The situation in which we are placed is, in debt and no money to pay and often without meat, also at times without bread, only oatmeal to subsist on, and this year all our crops have failed and all my property kept from me. I am seventy-two years of age and at my time of life to know the want of bread, of which I never did before, is truly painful."*

It is in these circumstances that 1836 slips away into 1837.

Winter in the New House
1837

In spite of creditors at the door the house is finished in the autumn and the family looks forward to winter nights in their own rooms, in front of their own warm fires.

Bone tired, many times, Mary wonders just how she possibly might turn the tide that seems to have no ebb. Her boys have proven their worth. They willingly attack anything that has to be done and they do it well but she knows that she can't leave them and go to England to pressure the lawyers to settle the Bridgwater and Sheerness properties and her other business affairs.

Political unrest in both Upper and Lower Canada adds new pressures to their life on the mountain. The quest for responsible government, to give power to the people and overthrow the rulings of the wealthy British, and, in Lower Canada, to demolish the seigneurial system that so controlled the Canadien farmers, brings about the conscription of all able bodied young men. Two groups quickly form in Canada; one which favours the status quo and one which demands reform in both Upper and Lower Canada.

William, because of his age, is compelled to serve with the Militia requiring him to be away from home for training. His family, secluded on the mountain, is quite safe but the people of St. Andrew's, early in the year, find the Rebels too close for comfort. The farmers arm themselves with pitchforks and scythes to protect their homes from being burned. The threat to Lachute being raided causes people to hide in cellars or shut down businesses and leave their homes to hide in the bush. Thankfully both these areas never suffer the devastation that they had feared.

The fighting was really not very far away. At St. Eustache the Rebel leader was killed and the men he led, hidden in the church, died when the Militia set fire to the building. The glow of the fire could be seen miles away in Carillon. It is a horrible moment in Canadian history.

Eight militia companies, with William included, were sent to St. Benoit where the Registry and other buildings were devastated by fire. William did his duty knowing that his weary mother and young siblings had no choice but to do his share of the work while he was away. Thankfully Richard was too young to serve.

With all this, Mary's sister-in-law gives her no peace. Betsey begs her to go to Montreal to finalize the shop business. Running a boarding house and visiting daily with her friend, Mrs. Scott, Betsey really does not seem to understand just how dire Mary's straits are. Surprisingly, on November 10th, flighty, impetuous Betsey takes it upon herself to go to England to settle everything! She leaves her children, even baby George, with her friend Mrs. Scott, and boards the steamship *British America* for Quebec City where she then boards the *Toronto* and *"sails through nothing but gales for 14 days."* London lawyers don't know what hit them! All she really learned was that her husband Ned owed two lawyers large sums of money going back twenty years. Thankfully she was able to convince them just how bad their circumstances are.

She spends Christmas and New Years with family and is not home on March 15th, 1837 when Mrs. Scott, fearing for little Georges' health calls Mary to Montreal. Mary cannot spare the money to travel by train and travels by horse over very bad roads causing both she and the animal to be completely exhausted.

> *"The horse, quite done up with good feeding and attention, is recovering. I wish I could say as much for the object of my journey. Poor George, I found him in a very weak state so much reduced, no trace of his former self remained. The fever broke for two days but returned and left the child in a state so weak that I fear all will be in vain. We must resign him to the will of the Almighty. The only satisfaction remaining to us is the consciousness of having done everything in our power for his restoration."*

In a few days the little boy has passed away.

Even away from home Mary worries and guides her flock.

> *"How has William managed to get the hams up? I saw a man yesterday, Holback, he tells me they will be good. Tell William, if it is possible, to get the rye straw home and feed the cattle with it. Richard says there is little hay left and that must be reserved for spring work. I fear we shall not have sufficient. Everything in Montreal is very dear. William I am sure will do all in his power."*

She tells them not to *"expect me 'til you see me."*

When Betsey returns May 9th, after a delightful voyage of six weeks, four months away from her family she relates that James and Ned, having not paid in twenty years owe £1000 to Mr. Anderson and that he will not allow Mr. Hunt to release any money.

She is distressed to hear of the death of her son and says she is *"indeed one of the most unfortunate, miserable creatures on earth, nothing but sorrow and trouble attends me, therefore like a Christian must endeavour to bear my loss."* Betsey is Betsey and now needs money to pay for her unsuccessful venture.

Michael Again, 1837

There is no indication that Michael ever visited the Byers home on the mountain but in England he did pass on news of Mary's plight and did try to solve the issue of Eliza's inheritance from her mother Ann's estate through her maternal Grandfather Stephenson. Again they had used their own money to improve the property and as a family decided to not release money until it sold and they got their money back. On a more positive side, if Eliza would create a Power of Attorney she would receive £20, plus interest, from her aunt who had lived at Whitby. Michael is willing to act as Power (of Attorney) for Eliza and do what he can for Mary to ease her burdens. If he is in London he promises to nudge Mr. Hunt into action. It never happened.

He says that "all is as when Mary left with politicians finding fault without being able to find a remedy. In the commercial world there has been great losses with the Yankies, who I think are not too honourable men."

But there is a light at the end of the tunnel. There is word of a general election. Princess Victoria is winning the hearts of her subjects and giving hope to all of Britain.

Excitement in Montreal

While visiting her Aunt Betsey in Montreal, Anne finds herself surrounded by the unfolding of history and sends the news back to the Mountain. Exciting things are happening.

The first steamship travelled from Montreal to Carillon making travel to Montreal on the Ottawa River much faster and easier.

The second event of note was a horrific steam vessel accident in New York City, explicitly described by the newspapers. Anne relates the tragic incident to her family back on the Mountain.

"The carelessness of the Captain keeping too much steam, in order to show his vessel off, passing the town, the boilers burst precipitating 190 to 200 unfortunate people to eternity. Limbs, blood and brains were dashed on the shore. The accident happened quite close to land. A few, that were in the Lady's cabin at the time, finding the boat a wreck, and overcome with fear, jumped into the water and were drowned before assistance could reach them. A little boy, in the extremity of despair, stood on the shore imploring the bystanders to save his father, mother and three sisters, who were struggling in the water, and he doomed to see drowned. Unfortunate boy, perhaps they were all the relations he had. The Captain was thrown in a dreadful state, dead upon the shore. It is a horrible tale to read. Dearly did he pay for his carelessness."

The next was even more exciting.

"The town (Montreal) is very gay now, nothing but red coats. All the regulars and the volunteers were reviewed by the Governor in person. We had a beautiful place on the parade ground close to the Generals. Three bands were playing most beautifully, the sun glancing on the bayonets. The happy faces around us, oh 'twas an exhilarating sight, the artillery drawn by such beautiful horses. The dress of the artillery men is the handsomest of all, in my opinion. While looking at the men sitting so fearlessly on those deadly engines of warfare, I almost doubted they could do much mischief. Returning from the review, we saw all the prisoners removed in coaches to the other gaol to take their trial. They looked dreadfully pale and haggard. It was shocking to see them smiling and laughing, endeavouring to appear unconcerned, when perhaps in a short time they may be no more. They were rebels."

Having been sent to the city to buy apple trees she knows she *"certainly shall have a deal of trouble with them"* before she gets them home.

The Death of Elizabeth Clarkson Dudderidge Huxtable

With the death of William, Mary had lost her rudder. With the death of her seventy-three year old mother in May, Mary lost her anchor. Over the years Elizabeth had always been there for her daughter. Her strength had become Mary's strength. Like her mother, Mary had become an astute businesswoman. The Fountain Inn, the Ship Chandler's Shop at 120 Cock Hill Ratcliff and the handling of William's affairs while he was at sea had trained her well. There had never been a time when Elizabeth had not been proud of her daughter's indomitable spirit. Over the last years she had prayed that her daughter would beat the seemingly unbeatable odds that now consumed her daily life.

Elizabeth's sons, James and Edward, had not inherited their mother's strengths. When they were young they often bypassed their mother to ask Mary for money when their mother said no. In later years, when the young men could not seem to keep their heads above water, like any mother, she helped in any way she could. In hindsight, perhaps Mary had helped too much.

Elizabeth Clarkson Dudderidge Huxtable died on the mountain and was buried on the mountain. No marker has been found to mark this courageous woman's resting place, although family tradition is that her remains were later moved to Hillside Cemetery at Hawkesbury.

Lawyers and Disappointments
1838

With Elizabeth gone, the quest for the family money in England and the settlement of her Canadian estate reached new heights. Letters to and from lawyers in England continue to cause frustration and hard feelings. Miriam still maintains that her husband, James, being the older son should claim the bulk of the money. Miriam and Mary, now neighbours on the mountain, are not always on speaking terms, thus making a negotiated settlement impossible.

Betsey's boarders have left her leaving her in dire straits and frightened by the danger of the war.

She writes as, fearfully, she watches from her window.

"Not only all this, we are in the midst of War! All had to leave Church on Sunday, the town in a most dreadful state of alarm. Cannons were placed at the Banks. The Volunteers were out with positive orders from Sir John to stop and search every person and vehicle that came in and out of Montreal. We have a double guard at our corner, as they are expected in from the Mountain. They are to shoot everyone who does not give a good account of themselves as Martial Law is proclaimed. Every inhabitant of Montreal is obliged to burn two candles in the second storey of their house from sunset to sunrise. There are no Carters or Canadiens to be seen in Montreal, not even in Church. They threatened to blow up the Town. Caughnawaga, St.Pierre, and another town are reported to have been burned by the Rebels.

At Beauharnois, they have 60 Royalist prisoners among whom are Mr. Ellice and Mr. Ross. Mrs. Ross and her niece being obliged to take refuge in the cellar. Mrs. Ellice is sister or niece to Lady Durham. At Acadia a child was stabbed to the heart in its mother's arms. Several widows have come in with their children, covered with blood, whose husbands they have murdered. All the loyal inhabitants of La Prairie had ten minutes' notice to quit. They have destroyed the Railroads and fired on the Steamboats.

I wish I was with you for God knows whether any of the devoted inhabitants here will live to see another summer. We are surrounded with, well-organized rebels. The Americans are prepared to join them and here is great talk."

The rebellion ended December, 7th, 1838. The British Military and the Loyalists were successful, hereby ending any possibility that the two Canadas would become republics. The people were granted concessions that took some powers from the wealthy, ruling British. Twenty-nine years later, without further combat, responsible government is granted by the passing of the British North America Act 1867. Government for the people by the people is now to be law.

One never knows what news will come from Montreal! Betsey and some of her family bid Mrs. Scott farewell when she sets sail for London and find themselves in an embarrassing predicament when they do not disembark before the ship leaves the dock. Maria writes.

"The sailors hearing there were three ladies on board, grumbled. Sadly it was quite impossible to lower any of the boats in consequence of the number of ships which surrounded us, or to drop anchor. They put tremendous large planks from the shore to try and reach the ship and about 20 gents stood on one end to steady it. Mama was then handed over the side and was in the very act of jumping from the ladder on the plank when the ship began to recede faster - which so frightened her that, languidly reclining her head on the shoulder of the very athletic sailor, allowed herself to be very quietly carried to shore."

When it came to Maria's turn it was said to be a great risk, but she had no choice and tells all.

"Only fancy to yourself how I must have looked standing there, 2 men holding my hands above my head, one holding my clothes and guiding my feet which Mr. Nagy was kneeling to receive, but

stretching himself too far over, he fell plump over his head into the water. He escaped with a good dunking and somehow or other I found myself in the midst of the laughing spectators and, to add to our distress the rain came down in torrents. Away we all took to our heels amidst the galloping of the horses, the swearing of the carters, the shouts and hurrahing of the sailors and the loud laughter of the gentlemen, and took refuge in a low, dirty public house full of soldiers who very politely handed us chairs and retired to the back of the room. Thus ended the disasters of that eventful morning."

A letter from Maria usually lightens the day.

1839

In 1839 Mary receives money from the settlement of her mother's Canadian estate, recouping part of her investment in the business of the shop on Notre Dame Street. Now if only the money in England can be settled. Life is not really getting any better but the family doggedly keeps going.

1840

It has been another hard year. Mary is now fifty years old. Brought up and educated in London and Sheerness, Kent, England, this genteel, young lady toured the continent. She was faithful to her Roman Catholic beliefs, kind, gentle, loving and loyal. Her undaunted spirit led her to sail, and, according to her husband, she was a good sailor. She had been tried to the limit by the deaths of two of beloved children in infancy. Now she is bone-tired and old before her time. She is forced to rest and this gives her some time to ponder her plight.

Her letter dated April 29, 1840, 7th Range Chatham, Lower Canada, to Mr. Neate, lawyer in England tells her true heart-wrenching story.

"Respected Sir,

Mary Byers McNabb

By a letter, which I received a few days since from my sister-in law, Mrs. E. Dudderidge, wherein she encloses a copy of yours of 7th of March, I am informed of the sale of the Sheerness property & of your & Mr. Cannon's wish and advice respecting a settlement of my affairs & that a letter was addressed by the latter gentleman to me confirmatory of your mutual opinion, which letter has never come to hand. I feel less reluctance in refusing to accede to your request, because I am confident could every circumstance be fully explained, neither of you would feel it either equitable or just in me to comply. I have a sacred duty to perform towards my children paramount to every other & which, with the blessing of God, I will never lose sight of. You who are both fathers, will I am sure form a just estimate of my feelings of Mr. Orme, and this subject, but you do not, cannot, know a tenth part of my sufferings here.

I have been reduced to toil from sunrise to sunset in the open fields under a scorching heat, not for a day, but for months every year save the last, to obtain a scanty supply of the common necessities of life. Sometimes, I thought my reason would have left me, but heaven spared me that affliction. My health gave way & obliged me to desist, yet not before my example had animated my children, who are by nature and education unfit for toil, to strain every nerve to gain comparative independence, which exertions have been far rewarded with success, that if our health be spared, we are now at least removed far above absolute want 'tho we must still work hard & who was it reduced us to all this, but my late dear unfortunate brothers, who broke their promise to us in every way. I wish not to disturb the ashes of the dead but, at this time, the truth must be spoken. It was to use my dear Mother's expression 'to see me righted' that my beloved Mother at her advanced age consented to leave her native country & sink at length, disappointed and broken hearted, into the grave. When I saw the earth close over her I felt alone. Save my children, I had none left. The best friend was taken from me, vilified and aspersed by those I had gone some length to serve. You will I trust, Sir, pardon this egotism.

Returning to the subject of your letter, I cannot for reason I have named give up the Bridgwater estate to anyone, neither will I consent to a division of property, thereby depriving my children of their birthrights, but will I abide by my late mother's Will. What I may do for the children hereafter is a different thing, but I hold out no promises. I shall act as my conscience dictated when all is settled.

Therefore Mr. Thomas Nicholls may spare himself the trouble of threatening me 'that if I do not consent my brother's creditors shall have it.' The day will, I trust, arrive when Mr. Hunt will no longer refuse to do me justice. Am quite confident if he had acted according to dictates of his own honourable feeling he would have done so long since and not denied the means of providing those comforts for my lamented Mother, which her age & infirmities demanded required. My consolation is this that she is now enjoying the bright reward of all her sufferings in the world in a blissful immortality.

When Mrs. Fuller (Miriam) left the woods her property was valued at six hundred pounds independent of the farm & Mrs. F. settled out that and one thousand pounds on her. Mrs. E Dudderidge's (Betsey) house in Montreal is I am told worth a thousand pounds, while mine is put up to sale would not realize much more than the original cost (one hundred pounds), in consequence of it being a backwoods settlement. All I could obtain has been expended in improvements on it & have consequently no funds whatever.

My mother left business with an accumulation of six thousand pounds placed out at interest, a part in Mr. George Clarkson's hands, one thousand in the hands of Mr. Orme, at the time an eminent distiller in the Borough, the rest in the public funds, also a sum with which she purchased the lease of a house at Church End, Finchley.

My maternal Uncle resided with us, allowing my mother, for his board, one hundred per annum. The latter gentleman died two years prior to our leaving England intestate, by which my mother became possessed of his property, administered to under £3000.

On my marriage in 1815 my mother came to reside with me, before which time my brothers had obtained nearly the whole of her property & subsequently the remainder, with the exception of eighty pounds, the sum advanced to me in six hundred pounds, the like sum left me by my Uncle Dudderidge for which she took a mortgage on the ship Success, which by interest accumulating from the time of my Uncle's death about the year 24 or 25 brought it to the amount specified & enabled me to enter into business, by which I supported myself and children, and gave them the best education in my power, for my lamented husband was unfortunate in his profession, but he was an honest and upright man in all his dealings. I forgot to mention that one of the above sums was settled on me and the children. It was my Mother's wish & intention that I should share equally with my brothers her property. They told us their stock would pay doubly all their debts & I strove by every means in my power to lessen my expenses, simply imagining that I was hoarding up for my children, in the hands of my brothers a comfortable provision. The results you are acquainted with.

I explain all this because Mrs. E.D. brought word in her return from England that my mother would be sent for to serve her claim on their property, which caused her great trouble. I owe two sums, debts of my own contracting in the way of my business, amounting to forty three pounds, which the moment I receive monies from England I shall pay & then that will be off my mind.

I once more beg to apologize for the great length of this letter & assure you how grateful I feel for your kindness in interesting yourself for me and mine and to assure you I am with much respect,

Yours sincerely & obliged

Mary Byers"

Mary does not receive a response to her plea for help. Where is this man and the other lawyers? Incompetence is an answer or perhaps someone has spent her security. Over time letters go back and forth, some are good others not.

Fourteen months later, 1841, with the settlement of her mother's suit, Clarkson and Steine, there is a promise of three or four hundred pounds but by November no money had arrived. Mr. Hunt is still holding it. Mary's spirits plummet and she tries again.

Respected Sir,

"I beg to acknowledge the receipt of your friendly letter wherein you promised a second favour in a month or so. My sons have anxiously enquired at the Post Office many times in vain. Let me hope that no further delay will occur, but that on receipt of this, you will perform your promise and be enabled to confirm the pleasing intelligence of the former 'that brighter days were in prospect for me.' Such a deep gloom has hung over me & mine for these last eight years that I can scarce believe it possible this is the month you named & I trust no unforeseen disappointments will intervene. The death of your Father you named must no doubt occupy much of tour time. I am doubly grateful for that proportion your benevolent feelings dedicate to my affairs & hope God will reward you for your good feeling you display in favour of one time has rendered but for you & Mr. Cannon, friendless. I trust Mr. Hunt will think it time to put an end to my sufferings which have been multiplied & without further delay come to a settlement. If I was to enter into particulars & you an account of all the privations we endure in these woods you could scarce credit my statement, but thank God it is no worse. We have all our crop safe, more than sufficient for family use & my boys are busy making potash to clear a small part of the debt we contracted last year.

I received a letter from Mr. Cannon, I was quite delighted to find myself in error respecting him, for I had without mercy consigned him to the tomb.

I fear we are going to have a long winter. There has been snow on the ground for these ten days and I think it will stay here. September is early for snow!"

When will all this end?

More Dudderidge News

During the summer of 1840 Mary and Betsey continue to communicate. For years, Betsey's son, Edward has lived with Mary on the mountain. He seems to be challenged in some way and difficult for his mother to handle. He has caused one problem too many and Mary is threatening to send him back to his mother. This is not acceptable because Betsey and Mr. King are to marry, August 27th. Only Mary and Anne are invited to the wedding, Edward is not welcome at this time. King, wary of meeting Mary, suddenly changes the wedding date. He probably knows that Mary has figured out that he has been an agitator in the quest for the Clarkson money and would rather not see her. Betsey feels that her new husband will do "*his best to contribute to her happiness and comfort for the future.*" She does not want her son to live with her so he does not, leaving good old Aunt Mary to deal with a new treatment for Edward's skin "*eruptions*".

> "*The Doctor says it is because Edward eats oatmeal so he is to refrain from it altogether, and to wash his body often with a solution of one spoonful of sulphur and one of quick lime to be boiled one quarter of an hour in a quart of water and to take occasionally a spoonful of sulphur as a medicine, to be very particular in keeping himself clean, and to have frequent changes of linen. It is nothing alarming.*"

Betsey has won again!

1842

In late September or early October Anne and her husband, William Stephens, give Mary her first grandson. A baby brings happiness to any home and Mary welcomes little William to the Mountain. A fire at the Stephens home at Cushing and ill feelings between Anne's husband and his parents have caused Ann and William to live indefinitely with Mary and the children. Indeed Anne remained in the same house until the Mountain property was sold.

More letters to and from London, to no avail, prompt Mary to give consent to Mr. Neate to pay himself the £100 he had advanced to Betsey and the £100 owed to Mr. Cannon thinking that perhaps these debts are the cause of their inaction. It did work only to find that *"Mr. Hunt has spent the money and has not got it to repay"*.

There is a bit of hope. Thomas Neate has settled another of Mary's mother's legal suits and though he did not get what was due he did send £200, having kept back the fees for his work. Thankfully, the money did reach the mountain.

Mary Dreams Again

£200 isn't much but it is a start and it gives Mary a bit of light at the end of the tunnel. Her body has been greatly challenged but her indomitable spirit and her faith allow her mind to dream again. She is part of a good community with helpful friends and neighbours. As she had seen before in England, she now sees no future for her boys here on this mountain. They are clever, strong and ambitious. She knows that there is more out there for them. Eliza and Anne are married and raising grandchildren for her to love. In time wee Mary and the boys will marry as well. Like her own mother had done for her she has educated and taught her daughters well. She will always guide them when needed but will let them live their chosen lives.

She has been told to rest and so she does in a comfortable chair under her favorite, tall pine tree where the familiar scent calms her soul. The view of the southern horizon seems to urgently call her name. How can she get off the mountain, leave Woodland Cottage and get on to an easier life? There is a river not an ocean to cross. She sees it as a leap of faith; one that her beloved husband, if he were here, would make with her.

She remembers how she and William had agreed that they did not want their sons to face a life on the seas. Surely, now he would agree that his dream of being a lumber baron on his mountain was not a dream his sons could follow. They have proved their worth and Mary knows they are both capable of carrying out dreams of their own. They love animals and any challenge to plant, tend and harvest their rewards. They need land, good land, a good water supply and space for the two young men to work amicably together and raise families of their own.

She will charge the boys with the task of asking questions when they cross the Ottawa River to take wood to the Hamilton Mills, in Hawkesbury. She is not adverse to leaving Lower Canada and moving to Upper Canada. Hopefully, someone will tell the boys of land for sale and how to get to see it.

As she rests, listening to the music of the wind through the tall pines, she thanks God for the kindness of her old childhood friend, John Cannon. When she left England she had had to leave behind her beloved piano. A whole new vista for the long winter presents itself when John Cannon sends a piano to the mountain. It is truly a miracle that her beloved piano has travelled from England across the Atlantic Ocean all the way to the wilderness. There is a message to be pondered and cherished. She is now in his debt for the amount of 20 shillings but with music and dreams they will lumber on, day by day, week by week until 1842 storms into 1843.

1843

March 21st, John Cannon urges Mary to divide the money equally with her sisters-in-law. If she does not she runs the risk of Mr. Hunt paying the money to the Court of Chancery, leaving nothing to have or to divide. Two bits of good news end his letter. The Bridgwater property has been sold and England has a new tariff allowing the importation of colonial wheat and flour at almost a nominal duty providing wider markets for Mary's grains. *"At 42 shillings per cwt. for butter & everything in proportion"*, she needs tillable land, lots of land!

Having no choice Mary agrees with her friend and easily reaches an agreement with Miriam, but feels that Mrs. King, Betsey, still needs to honour the debt of £120 plus £242, 10 shillings due to be divided among Edward's children but used by their mother. A family settlement cannot be reached leaving the conclusion in the hands of the lawyers in England. Time is wasted again. In the end Mr. King is most disappointed with the amount paid out to his wife.

The 18th of July 1843, a legal document of the Province of Canada signed by Miriam and her husband, Rinaldo Fuller, a farmer in Chatham, assured Mary that 28 pounds, 10 shillings paid to this sister-in-law cleared all claim on Elizabeth Huxtable's estate, meaning also money from England.

The Road to Fenham Farm

On good advice, William and Richard scout for land across the Ottawa River and make their way to Brown's Corners (Green Lane), a community half way between Hawkesbury and Vankleek Hill, Ontario. There is land to buy and it sells itself to them. From the road they see a plateau of land sloping to the west with a lie in to the east. They venture forth and find trees and more trees; tall evergreens and magical, shading umbrellas edging gentle slopes and flat spans of billowing grasses. Someone has recently cut a vast amount of timber but this is not necessarily a negative, it does provide acreage immediately inviting someone to build or cultivate. Sparkling, clear spring water ripples in a wandering way across a wide span and follows the base of the mid-central high plain making its way down a gentle, winding path through dense green cedars to join more bubbling brooks and splash over smooth stepping stones. It seems to call one to follow, to see just how far this unharnessed water will go.

The young men know that their mother must see what they have found and when she does she agrees; they have done well. She can't possibly hear, but perhaps she can, that there seem to be voices calling her to come and build and create a haven for her family and a home for generations yet to come. The land is not at all rocky. They have had enough rocks to last a lifetime. The slopes are gentle but distinct enough to beckon skis and sleds for winter fun. Someday she will tell her grandchildren of the winters on the mountain, the winter wonderland that kept her family sane.

Feeling that her prayers are answered she immediately begins the process of acquiring this bit of Eden meant for her sons. Early in 1843, Mary buys prime land in the Township of West Hawkesbury, Prescott County, Upper Canada. Deal making of any kind is seldom easy and this one is complicated. She deals with Mr. R. N. Watts, a landowner from Drummondville in Lower Canada, who also happens to be a member of the Legislature of the United Canadas situated in Montreal. He is acting for his brother, Captain John James Watts of Walmer Castle, England, a gentleman who has inherited this large block of from his late aunt, Mrs. Margaret Lake. Many letters go back and forth but a deal for 15 shillings, or three dollars an acre is amicably made.

Because the transfer papers for the north half of lots 13 and 14 will take some time to reach Fenham, Mary asks that she may take immediate possession as several persons have been plundering valuable timber and will likely be at it again in the winter. Four groups of squatters who have built several small buildings, claiming illegal residency, will also have to be dealt with. Permission was given along with an offer of more adjoining land. Everything progresses well and Mary is pleased.

A letter from daughter Mary to Mother Mary, dated May 6, 1843, to the new Post Office in Chatham finds young Mary, William and Richard living in a *"shanty"* on the new property.

"My Dear Mother,

It is with great pleasure I sit and for the first time address a few lines to you, hoping that it will find you all well as it leaves us at present. I long to see you all. Has the baby got any more teeth? He surely runs by this time.

I have got quite domesticated in the little shanty. It begins to look somewhat like home. There is a great many invitations pouring in. We have a great many evening calls from the young ladies which I have to return.

Beauty is not going to calf until August which will prove a great disappointment. It is a very pretty place where the house is going to be built. There is neither stump nor stone and a place for a garden close to it. I can assure you, you will be pleased with it.

I had almost forgotten to ask if Anne had weaned little William. What would I not give to see you all, but thank God, one month has gone by. Write me a long letter. Tell me all that has passed at home, since I last saw you, not forgetting old pets.

I hope my time will come. I shall be very happy to welcome you to our humble lot when you honour us with a visit in the summer. Do you think my silk bonnet would alter? I don't know what to do about it. I think it a pity to wear my straw one on every occasion.

I must conclude for want of more to say. William joins me in kind love to yourself, dear Anne, and all the children. A dozen kisses for little William.

May God bless you, my dear Mother, and keep up your spirits, I remain your affectionate daughter,

Mary Dudderidge Byers"

The young people have landed on their feet. Their new neighbours, the Higginson's, next door at Emerald Hill, have welcomed them warmly, helped in any way possible, with kindness, knowledge and labour, forming friendships that have lasted through many generations.

Two young Higginson men, John and George, who have already planned and built houses and barns, organize a bee and by June 22nd a "*new design*" house is raised; the first Byers home on Fenham.

Daughter Mary tells her mother, who is still living with Anne and William Stephens at Woodland Cottage that, having lost a baby turkey, to keep the remaining nine babies safe with the mother turkey hen, she has tied the mother's leg to a stump; they have two young colts and old Kate has a young filly. She is trying so hard to manage this grown-up role that she finds herself in. She reminds her Mother to gather flower seeds to create familiar gardens and that friends have promised "*snow balls*" and many other flowers. In my time Snow Balls still grow at Fenham.

As is promised the new house is ready by Christmas and Mary leaves Woodland Cottage and mountain life behind. She is filled with pride. No three young people could have done any better. Life on the mountain had trained them well. There was much to do but they were happy with new friends and beauty all around them.

The money cloud will not go away. News that Betsey's husband has tried to have an advance of money has induced Mr. Hunt, Mary's lawyer to dig in his heels. Again he stresses that they must all agree or risk getting nothing. One lawyer, Mr. Anderson, having been in prison a very long time and just released must also agree to all that is to be done leaving John Cannon frustrated with his peers.

1845

By January 17, 1845 John Cannon seems to be very tired of Mary's business. She really can't blame him, many would have given up long ago. Finally all the lawyers have agreed that the money is "Mary's alone" but she will still have unsettled business with Betsey. She prays that a quick solution will lead to her extended family living harmoniously in the years to come. She knows that her mother would want the animosity to end.

John Cannon ends thus,

> "*I placed to your credit as per account annexed and have paid the balance to the North American Bank here to be paid you at Montreal. A letter of credit is enclosed for £390 of which*

arrangement I hope you will approve, as I am convinced I have acted for your interest in every way. In any arrangements you may make with the Fullers you must abate the £25 as paid Nichols on their account. I can only say now the concern is settled that I never had a business on hand that has given me so much trouble and anxiety, and at one time I despaired of ever bringing it to a conclusion. Neither is Mr. Hunt been to blame. You must remember that the other parts of the family have been as urgent on him as myself, each considering themselves entitled to it.

Am happy to see by your letter how much better your prospects are than formerly. I sincerely hope your good success will increase. I should be happy to have my young friends as correspondents and receive from them consignments of wood goods or anything else that may be beneficial to them. It seems but a short time, although so many years have passed and changes occurred, hope for better times. Expecting that we used to meet as boys and girls in Cannon Road and Tower Hill, and many, many pleasant evenings have we passed together with those who are now no more. I often talk over them with my dear children. They are all quite well and desire their kind remembrances. Business still continues very dull and I find much ado to live but hope to hear from you by return."

Mary is humbled by her friend's loyalty and perseverance. Hopefully she never needs or sees another lawyer but it is not meant to be.

In April the agreement with Miriam is found to be faulty in that her husband's lawyer has cleverly manipulated words leaving a loop hole that the Fullers will use to take action against Mary when the money is paid out. They do not intend to give up what they see as the older son's share of Mrs. Huxtable's money. Mary did not win this suit. March 30th, 1847, Mary's son, William or WEN as he was known, was made to pay £238 pounds to Miriam's husband, Rinaldo Fuller. It was not until August 21, 1848 that Mary's brother's two sons, James Edward and Richard C. Dudderidge finally signed off on their grandmother Elizabeth's will, at last granting their Aunt Mary some peace.

August 1845, eight years after Elizabeth Huxtable's death, Mary seeks settlement of her mother's Canadian will and gets this reply, *"It is rather soon for you to become impatient that your affairs should be brought to a conclusion for the court in which the business lies has not sat since the 30th of July and law business is slow".*

In dismay she wonders why she should be surprised. This time it is a Mr. Hoyle in Montreal. They all seem tarred with the same brush.

There is more to the world than money matters. Two land issues have to be resolved. First the matter of Captain Brown, a neighbour, whose determination to continue cutting trees on Mary's land has to be settled. Hoping to do so, December 14, 1846, Mary writes to Mr. Watts,

> *"By your authority, we took possession of the land and put up notices warning people to keep off, when Captain Brown, who resides in the neighbourhood, put up a notice claiming possession by Power of Attorney granted him by Sir John Johnson, dated April 1822, by which he is empowered to preserve the timber, instead of which, with the Power of Attorney no longer valid, he has taken off all the valuable timber. Last winter he took, according to report, upwards of four hundred saw logs and now forbids us to 'cut a stick'. I wish to know whether that Power still holds good to Captain Brown."*

The answer was a positive one. Having refused Mr. Brown's offer to buy said lands at 10 shillings an acre and assuring Mary that no Power of Attorney in favour of Captain Brown exists, Mr. Watts gives her power to claim from Mr. Brown the value of the stolen logs.

> *"You are to have the benefit of any monies that may be recovered from him or others for logs or timber taken from these lands since 1836."*

Mr. Brown did not give up easily causing Mr. Watts to take a firmer step.

On January 20, 1847, Mr. Watts writes to Mr. Brown,

"Begging reference to the letter I addressed to you a few days since, I beg to inform you that unless you immediately desist from trespassing on my half of Lot 13 and 14 in the 3rd Concession of West Hawkesbury, I shall institute proceedings against you, as also I require an immediate settlement to Mrs. Byers for the timber you have taken."

Annoyed, Mr. Watts tells Mary,

"In conveying to you the land, I will also convey the claim against Captain Brown and give you all the powers I am invested in the Power of Attorney to collect the same from them."

This is definitely good news.

Mr. Watts has power to sell another 100 acres, the rest of lot 13 and the deal is made for 12 shillings 6 pence per acre. He has a great deal of trouble understanding the division of lots in Upper Canada. In Lower Canada they are divided lengthways, long and narrow, while in Upper Canada they are divided across making them more compact. Mary is able to make him understand and all is well.

By mid-February Mary has paid the £75 for the north halves of Lots 13 and 14 and even though she doesn't want it offers 2 dollars an acre for the last 100 acres in the south half of Lot 14 that Mr. Watts is most anxious to sell. Even though much of Lot 14 is a wetland the firewood it will provide will be a great asset in enabling the clearing of other forest to improve the farm. Now having the land free from all encumbrances she takes a stand on the matter of the squatters, expecting again a positive reply.

"I find I have not mentioned the squatters on the lands, there being one on ½ Lot 13 of the name of Robert Bruce, which Captain Elijah Brown gave liberty to settle there better than 4 years ago. He has built a sound log house and made very little clearance, and as I buy the land free from all encumbrances, it is your part to dispossess him, and there is one on the 100 acres of Lot 14, which I now make an offer for, named Joseph Gload, and I believe another, but as the line is not run I am not certain."

Really the answer is just what Mary needs. She is more than fed up waiting for others to settle her problems. The trespasser will be gone very quickly!

Mr. Watts' reply suffices.

> *"As far as squatters are concerned, your family being on the spot, you will be enabled to communicate with the Sheriff so much more readily than I could that I must leave that part of the business to your attention."*

Communicate they did and the Sheriff soon solved the problem and life settled down on the 480 acres which now constituted Fenham Farm.

Semi-Retirement for Mary

It is time to give the boys their wings. William is 24 and Richard is 20, still young, but both having proven their capabilities, Mary is ready to give them more latitude to create their own destiny, always cognisant that, as their mother, she will remain their anchor of wisdom and support. It will still be a great deal of hard work for the little party who left Woodland Cottage on the mountain. William and Richard have never turned their backs on hard work. Young Mary, an avid gardener, has already made her mark on the property maintaining a thriving garden, an impressive collection of fruit-bearing bushes and an orchard that is already beginning to bear fruit. The competence of her children means she now has some time to explore new possibilities and build as she wishes. Life is good! The dream is beginning to take form.

Emerald Hill, a well-established farm east of Fenham, is the home of the William Higginson family, a large family, with capable young women and several energetic young men, who continue to be the source of wise advice and generous talent and labour.

Mary is excited to witness the friendship that is developing between her elder son William (WEN) and Ellen, the eldest of the Emerald Hill family. It would be so wonderful if William and Ellen were to marry. She will do her best to nurture this friendship.

It was all the more exciting because Jane Tweed Higginson, Ellen's mother, is becoming her very dearest friend. Years ago Mary had had many special friends, in London, in Sheerness, at Tusmore and even in Antigua. The years in the mountain have given little time for making friends. She has missed having a good friend and confidante. Thankfully the empty spot in her life is beginning to be filled. Emerald Hill's matriarch, the indomitable Jane Tweed Higginson, is becoming her soulmate, confidante and most loyal friend. Next door neighbours, they will grow old together.

1847

By 1847 the potato famine in Ireland had destroyed the lives of many Irish families causing huge numbers of impoverished, starving people to emigrate to Canada in what became known as coffin ships because so many people perished from disease in their fetid holds. Many children were orphaned. In Quebec City and Montreal orphanages were crowded with these unfortunate children. Those who came from Protestant families were gathered together at the Montreal Protestant Orphans' Asylum, where caring matrons sought to find suitable homes for them with Protestant families.

The call went out from the city for homes. At Fenham it was obvious that there was a need for more hands. The children needed homes, and love, and good food. Mary felt sure that William and Richard would be good mentors for a young boy who would have to make his way in the world without his parents' guidance. In January 1848, Mary sent William to Montreal to bring home a fourteen year old, James Kerr, to live at Fenham.

James and his sister, Esther, had been orphaned when their mother died of ship's fever at the quarantine station located at Grosse Ile below Quebec City. The family had proceeded on from Quebec City to Montreal, where their father also died, another victim of the terrible disease which raged in that city.

Upon learning that James has a sister, Mary immediately makes plans to reunite the children. She contacts the ophanage but fate gets in the way and before Esther can be picked up she is given to another family. The siblings never meet again. James becomes a member of the family until 1854 when he leaves to work for the Hamilton Brothers in the shanties along the Rouge River. James and his wife, Ann Jane Potter, purchased a farm near Vankleek Hill, and became the patriarch and matriarch of a fine family.

Time Marches On

Over time barns and houses are built. The faint remains of a foundation just west of the entrance from the road suggests that perhaps it was the base of the shanty where William, Richard and their sister Mary had lived as they began to carve out their new dream. In time it may have been moved to a spot just west of the current house where years of leaves seemed to cover the faint remnant of a structure.

From 1859 to 1864 the three 200 acre lots on the Mountain were each sold for £50 pounds and by 1864 the remaining mountain property no longer belonged to the Byers family. The trials and tribulations of the years without their Captain William had served to strengthen both Mary and her crew. The city lady had overcome all odds and fostered a work ethic in her children that could not be bettered by anyone.

The young men worked very well together. Before long both were ready to begin families of their own. On May 3, 1849, William married Ellen Higginson and the Fenham family was forever welded to the Emerald Hill Higginson's from next door.

In 1850 Richard married Mary Ann Owens from Stonefield, Quebec, and Mary married William Thorn Higginson, the son of George Higginson from Burnside, the farm immediately to the south of Fenham.

So much has changed for Mary, but it is good change. All of her children are now married and she looks forward to more grandchildren. William and Ellen are settled into their new home on Constitution Hill. She will make her

154

home with Richard and Mary Ann. In truth, she knows that she will also be spending time with Mary and William Higginson and with Anne and William Stephens. She knows her Captain would approve. How she wishes he were here to share her joy.

William and Richard continue to share Fenham. Wisely, Mary divides the land giving the front half to Richard and the rear half to William. It seems like an odd arrangement until you realize that each son would have a share of the higher land to the east and the lower land to the west. Land is being cleared and put into production as Fenham emerges from the wilderness. Both couples are producing children as the new generation of Mary and the Captain's family comes into being.

In 1859, William and Richard dissolve their partnership when Richard and Mary Ann decide to move back to Lower Canada to be nearer to her family. William takes over Richard's land and the property remains in his family's care for the next 117 years.

Richard and his young family establish a farm near Lachute, Lower Canada for the next 10 years, then move to a farm at L'Orignal Ontario for a short time. In 1873, leaving his wife and family behind, Richard and his second son, William Dudderidge Byers, go west to homestead in Manitoba. They acquire land near Portage la Prairie and return to the east the following year to move the rest of the family to their new home on the prairie.

With her children all established in their own homes and with many, many grandchildren, Mary had the freedom, at last, to enjoy the vocation of grandmother and pursue a quieter, well- earned retirement. She was known to frequently leave Fenham to spend time with her other children, to bond with newly born grandchildren and the older children who loved the attention she afforded them. She visited family and friends in Montreal, always being aware of the life at Fenham.

Life was good, neighbours were good. Fenham was an important part of the farming community.

The Big Barn at Fenham c. 1890
(Byers family collection)

The House at Fenham
(Byers family collection)

William Edward Nelson Byers
(McGibbon Photography, Hawkesbury, Ont)

Richard Dudderidge Byers
(Browne & Co., Hawkesbury & Vankleek Hill, Ont)

Autumn at Fenham Farm 1875

The breeze is light. The ripened wheat in the front field waves with the breeze, its golden hues, a sea of motion, in the late afternoon sun. Soothed by the rhythm of the gleaming sea, Mary, now 82, sits to rest and enjoy the splendour and the brilliance of the September colour. From her rocking chair on the front veranda, the rolling Laurentian Hills, the mountains that once caused so many tears, now resplendent in all their glory, say "peace". She feels peace. Life has been a journey of happiness and sorrow with hardships beyond belief, but one that has brought her to this beautiful home, the culmination of her dreams. She knows that William must be very proud of what she and her children have accomplished in the Fenham he dreamed of so many years ago.

In her hands she holds a tiny, open, red leather case. The oval glass protects a small miniature of her beloved husband. He was so young and handsome in his dark mariner's uniform. She remembers how worried she had been when news of a bad storm told her of the loss of his right eye. Gazing at his face she sees no imperfection. Only courage and love speak to her. She turns the keepsake over again, to admire the tiny pearls that surround a lock of his dark hair, a curl that reminds her of the soft, caring man who now, at times, is almost a dim memory.

She has had a busy day. There was a time when it would have been difficult to imagine that someday she would do only what she wanted to do, but here she was doing just that. The morning had been spent gathering butternuts that had fallen from trees not far from the house. She and her competition, the squirrels, enjoy each other; chattering conversations echo through the trees. Her busy friends seem to know that she will never take more than her share.

She naps in her chair to awaken refreshed and ready to scatter her morning bounty on wooden racks lovingly crafted by her twelve year old grandson Charles. The nuts must dry and be turned regularly until they are ready to be cracked and the meat carefully extracted. They will end up in much anticipated delicious baking and candy. Christmas in not Christmas without butternuts from Fenham.

How farfetched it would have been when she was young to believe that one day she would talk to the squirrels at Fenham Farm. She could not possibly know that the squirrels of Green Lane could never claim a monopoly on butternuts until her great grandson Charles, lovingly known as Carol, passed away on May 13th, 1995.

The seasons pass quickly and her rheumatism seems to slow her down a little more each year. She misses Richard and his family so far away in Portage la Prairie, Manitoba but, true to form, her love of letter writing and the faithful responses allow her to feel part of their lives.

It is December 1875, her Christmas messages have all been written to her western family and to family and friends in Quebec. She hopes that, if weather permits, over the festive season she will see all those living close by. Her wish comes true. She is blessed with one more wonderful, family Christmas Day.

January 1876

1876 brings grief to Fenham Farm. Grandmother Mary has a terrible accident. She falls down the front stairs, is badly injured and passes away on January the fifth.

January 23rd, Richard in Camp Creek, Manitoba receives the sad news and writes back home to his brother William.

> *"I am in receipt of yours of the 5th containing the melancholy intelligence of the death of our poor Mother, also one written a few days before that sad event describing the serious fall she had down the stairs. It is sad to think that her death should have been hastened by an accident, but we must not repine, for that and all other events are directed by a superior intelligence.*

Poor Mother! She had many severe trials through life, under all of which she acted the part conscientiously. In fact, I think few have passed through so long a lease of life so consistently. This should be a source of consolation to us for it justifies the belief that she will meet her reward in the next world.

Indeed, I cannot tell you for you can imagine, how I grieve to think that I could not have seen her once more before she departed but I trust we shall meet again in another and a better world.

I remain ever your affectionate Brother,

Richard D Byers"

Mary lay at rest in the front parlor of her dream home at Fenham. Her journey had been long; a memorable one that ended as it should with deep gratitude, celebrated with love by her family and friends.

> *"Mary Dudderidge Byers*
> *beloved wife of*
> *Captain William Byers*
> *dear mother of*
> *William Edward Nelson Byers*
> *Anne Byers Stephens*
> *Richard Dudderidge Byers*
> *Mary Dudderidge Byers Higginson*
> *respected step-mother of*
> *Elizabeth Stephenson Byers Wilson*
> *completed her earthly journey at*
> *Fenham Farm, Hawkesbury, Ontario, Canada*
> *January 5, 1876"*

She rests beside William, on the top of a hill, overlooking the Ottawa River, in Hillside Cemetery, Hawkesbury, Ontario, Canada.

Mary Byers McNabb

The Author's Thoughts

One hundred years and more, good times and bad, never weakened the love and respect the people of Fenham felt for a heritage, so long ago carved with hard work, love and dreams.

Without Mary and the Captain's letters there would be no story to tell, no seas to sail, no storms to worry about, no shipwrecks to survive and no dreams that firstly found lasting love and secondly carried the spirit of the family to venture to a new world.

How different Mary's life would have been if William had not died? I believe that there still would have been a Fenham Farm. There was too much energy in the sons to stay on the mountain.

The letters did not tell us why the farm was named as it was but we do know that Fenham is a suburb of Newcastle in Northern England and we know that there are Byers people still in that area. We know that there was a Byers Castle, an estate, lost to the family when Nicholas Byers stayed true to the Jacobite cause after the defeat of King James ll. Legend tells that the seven generations of Byers Captains who had sailed from Shields and Sunderland were somehow connected to this property, perhaps a British Fenham Farm.

Along with the letters the many treasures left behind by the Success could, if they were able, tell many a harrowing tale. The bell, engraved with the name Success and dated 1803, graced the belfry of the carriage house/work shop and served the Captain's family for years. It was a privilege to be allowed to pull the rope and to hear its call. The barometer, spy glass, corner washstand, sextant and personal property of the Captain had sailed many voyages with the able Mariner and today are valuable, cherished family antiques.

Mary's faith carried her through the good and the bad. Without her courage, strength and determination she might have faltered somewhere along the way. Like her mother did for her, she endowed her children with good morals and her belief in a Mighty Power.

162

She was a daughter, sister, wife, mother, grandmother, friend and a very beautiful lady.

She was the anchor of the Fenham Farm Family.

In the summer of 2016, a family group, including my daughter Wendy, visited "The Mountain". The location became real to us when we noticed that the clearing was ringed with old, big apple trees. Page 134 of this book, tells the story of how apple trees got to "The Mountain".

My Brother Bill's book *"For Everything There is a Season..."* carries the Byers story over many more years and gives promise of more to come.

The Byers Family

First Generation

Captain William Byers, Sr. & Ann Nicholson

Second & Third Generations

Captain William Byers, Jr. & Anne Stephenson

Elizabeth Stephenson Byers & Robert Wilson

Captain William Byers, Jr. & Mary Dudderidge

Mary Byers (died in infancy)

William Edward Nelson Byers & Ellen Higginson

Anne Byers & William Stephens

Richard Dudderidge Byers & Mary Anne Owens

Mary Dudderidge Byers & William Thorn Higginson

Charles Byers (died in infancy)

The Clarkson/Dudderidge Family

First Generation

Henry Clarkson & Mary Nivum

Second & Third Generations

George Clarkson

Rev. William Clarkson

Elizabeth Clarkson & Richard Dudderidge

Mary Dudderidge & Captain William Byers

James (Jem) Dudderidge & Miriam Nicholls

Edward (Ned) Dudderidge & Elizabeth (Betsey) Clarkson

Elizabeth Clarkson & Anthony Huxtable

Elizabeth Huxtable (died in childhood)

Special Thanks

To my brother, Bill Byers, who generously gave me copies of the letters, talked with me for hours, spent numerous hours correcting my unacceptable typing and computer skills and enabled me to have a manuscript beautifully formatted and edited.

To my cousin, John Byers, who when he knew that I was bogged down, provided research material, sat with me and read and edited my work. He expertly provided the photos for the story and kindly acquired the rights to use "The Sheerness Picture".

To my Nephew, Ian McNabb who, frequently "fixed my computer" and, "just in case", saved my work on his system. His many hours put into publishing my work is much appreciated.